THE AUSTRALIAN Women's Weekly

VEGAN

THE AUSTRALIAN **Women's Weekly**

VEGAN

NUTRITIOUS, DELICIOUS
PLANET-FRIENDLY MEALS

Project Editor Siobhán O'Connor
Project Designer Alison Shackleton
Editor Lucy Sienkowska
Jacket Designer Alison Donovan
Jackets Coordinator Jasmin Lennie
Production Editor David Almond
Production Controller Rebecca Parton
Managing Editor Dawn Henderson
Managing Art Editor Alison Donovan
Art Director Maxine Pedliham
Publishing Director Katie Cowan

First published in Great Britain in 2023
by Dorling Kindersley Limited
DK, One Embassy Gardens, 8 Viaduct Gardens, London, SW11 7BW

The authorized representative in the EEA is Dorling Kindersley
Verlag GmbH. Arnulfstr. 124, 80636 Munich, Germany

Copyright © 2023 Dorling Kindersley Limited
A Penguin Random House Company
10 9 8 7 6 5 4 3 2 1
001–333815–Mar/2023

A CIP catalogue record for this book is available from the British Library.
ISBN: 978-0-2415-9822-1

Printed and bound in China

For the curious
www.dk.com

Contents

Plant-based living

A vegan diet is wholly plant-based and excludes all animal products. In addition to the obvious – no meat, seafood, eggs, or dairy products – honey, honeycomb, and gelatine are also off-limits. There are also a few surprising places that animal products can lurk, so remember to check labels first if you are unsure.

So what is a vegan diet?

Veganism is sometimes characterized as restrictive, difficult, and just plain hard work. But instead of focusing on what vegans don't eat, let's look at the abundance of ingredients vegans can enjoy. If you aren't already practising a vegan diet, it is not so hard to make the leap when you know that the array of foods that will fuel your day is expansive and often incorporates common ingredients. Best yet, a vegan diet doesn't mean giving up great-tasting food:

LEGUMES Dried and canned lentils, chickpeas, cannellini beans, kidney beans, black-eyed peas, borlotti beans, and green and yellow split peas.

GRAINS AND GRAIN SUBSTITUTES/PSEUDO-GRAINS Includes amaranth, barley, buckwheat, freekeh, oats, rice, farro, millet, polenta, quinoa, and wheat-based products such as flours, couscous, and bulgur wheat.

NUTS AND SEEDS Almonds, cashews, peanuts, pecans, pistachios, macadamias, walnuts, sunflower seeds, pumpkin seeds, linseeds (flaxseeds), chia seeds, and sesame seeds, as well as unhulled and hulled tahini.

SOY PRODUCTS Such as tofu, tempeh, and other soy products, including miso paste and 'cheeses'.

ALTERNATIVE, DAIRY-FREE MILKS There is a wide range of milks now available, including soy milk, rice milk, almond milk, coconut milk, and oat milk.

SEA VEGETABLES Includes seaweeds such as kelps, dulse, nori, kombu, and wakame, as well as spirulina.

HERBS AND SPICES Keep a ready supply of dried spices on hand in your pantry, including cardamom, cinnamon, cloves, coriander, cumin, fennel seeds, garam masala, garlic powder, ginger, mustard seeds and powder, nutmeg, onion powder, paprika, and turmeric. Fresh herbs such as basil, coriander, dill, flat-leaf parsley, mint, oregano, rosemary, and thyme all add flavour and freshness.

CONDIMENTS Including soy sauce, tamari, miso, vinegars, mustards, and nutritional yeast flakes.

Your nutritional needs

When planning vegan meals, especially when starting out, the most frequently asked questions are about how to incorporate all the necessary nutrients into your diet. To help avoid potential deficiencies, here are the most common nutrients that cause concern, together with suggestions for vegan sources to meet your dietary needs:

CALCIUM In place of dairy products, use nuts, seeds, leafy green vegetables, legumes, and soy products, especially those that are fortified with calcium.

IODINE Include sea vegetables such as nori, kombu, or wakame, and small amounts of iodized salt. Check with your doctor before taking supplements if you have a thyroid issue.

IRON Eat nuts, lentils, oats, dried fruit, dark leafy green vegetables, and soy products. Eating these in tandem with fresh foods rich in vitamin C aids the body in better absorbing the iron.

VITAMIN C Include tomatoes, red peppers, broccoli, citrus fruits, and berries in your diet.

OMEGA-3 FATTY ACIDS Include linseeds, chia seeds, pumpkin seeds, seaweed, spirulina, and walnuts.

PROTEIN Eat legumes, whole grains, quinoa, nuts, seeds, and soy products, especially tofu and tempeh.

VITAMIN B12 As this vitamin is found naturally only in meat, some fish, dairy, and eggs, make sure to incorporate foods fortified with vitamin B12, such as some cereals, plant-based milks, and soy products. A supplement can be taken for healthy blood cells.

ZINC Add whole grains, nuts, pumpkin seeds, wheatgerm, and soy products, especially tofu and tempeh to your diet.

Your day on a plate

ACTIVE PERSON If you fall into this category, especially if you are female and premenopausal, it is vital to eat as varied a diet as possible and avoid restrictive eating patterns, or you risk an inadequate dietary intake for optimum health. For the active vegan, incorporate energy-dense foods such as nuts, tofu, tempeh, and other quality protein at every meal. As vegetable proteins don't include all the necessary amino acids required, it is necessary to combine a variety of proteins throughout the day. Plant-based proteins are not as easily digested as meat-derived ones, so it is advised that vegans consume 10% more per day. If you are vegan and super-active, it is especially important to target iron-rich foods and monitor your iron stores. To ensure sufficient calcium intake, look for calcium-rich vegan foods such as almonds, leafy greens, and broccoli.

MODERATELY ACTIVE PERSON The nutritional requirements of a moderately active person are very similar to that of an active person. The main difference between the two is that your overall kilojoule requirements will be less. Also, your carbohydrate requirements may be reduced. As with a vegan diet in general, balance and eating widely from all plant-based foods are key to ensuring you capture vital nutrients and are not missing out on certain nutritional requirements that can be harder to meet in a vegan diet. Be aware, too, that many vegan foods are not necessarily healthy. In fact, manufactured vegan substitutes can be laden with not-so-useful bulking agents that add unnecessarily to your kilojoule quota. Also, just because a sweet treat is vegan doesn't afford it health-food status!

WAKE UP

Sweet or savoury, energy-boosting or indulgent, there are breakfasts here for every day of the week, from satisfying mueslis to irresistible pancakes and waffles.

Turmeric tofu scramble

PREP + COOK TIME **15 MINUTES** | SERVES **2**

Tofu is an excellent source of calcium, and a 100g serving of tofu will also provide you with 8g of protein, making this dish an energy-giving start to the day. It also works well for a weekend brunch or even a casual lunch with family or friends.

250g firm tofu

2 tsp nutritional yeast flakes (optional) (see tips)

$1/2$ tsp ground turmeric

$1/2$ tsp cumin seeds

$1/4$ tsp smoked paprika

2 tbsp extra virgin olive oil

4 spring onions, thinly sliced

1 garlic clove, crushed

1 tbsp coarsely chopped flat-leaf parsley

1 tbsp lemon juice

4 bagels, split, toasted

$1/3$ cup (85g) chipotle hummus (see tips)

2 tomatoes (300g), sliced

50g baby spinach leaves

$1/2$ cup (25g) mangetout tendrils or other pea shoots

salt and freshly ground black pepper

1 Pat the tofu dry with kitchen paper, to remove excess moisture. Using your hands, crumble the tofu into a small bowl. Set aside.

2 Combine the nutritional yeast flakes (if using), turmeric, cumin seeds, smoked paprika, and 1 tablespoon water in a small bowl; season with salt and pepper to taste.

3 Heat the olive oil in a medium frying pan over a medium-high heat; cook the spring onions and garlic for 1 minute or until softened. Add the crumbled tofu; cook, stirring, for 4 minutes or until the tofu starts to brown a little. Add the spice mixture; cook, stirring, for 1 minute or until the tofu is completely coated in the spices. Stir in the parsley and lemon juice until combined.

4 Spread the toasted bagel halves with the hummus; top the bases with the tomato, scrambled tofu, spinach leaves, and pea shoots. Sandwich with the top halves of the bagels to serve.

TIPS

- As a seasoning, nutritional yeast flakes provide a moreish, cheese-like umami taste. Look for a brand that is fortified with B12, an essential vitamin that is found naturally in meat, fish, dairy, and eggs, and therefore needs to be supplemented in a vegan diet.
- To add a smoky flavour to the scrambled tofu, simply use smoked tofu. You could also choose other spicy flavoured hummus such as jalapeño hummus or harissa hummus instead of chipotle.
- Top with other greens such as rocket and watercress, if you like.

Chocolate pancakes with maple banana

PREP + COOK TIME **20 MINUTES + STANDING** | SERVES **2**

Some flavour pairings are considered classics for a reason: they are very hard to resist.
Chocolate and banana definitely fall into this category. The treat factor is increased by
caramelizing the bananas in a little maple syrup first, before using them to top the pancakes.

2 tbsp vegetable oil

2 small bananas (260g)

2 tbsp pure maple syrup, plus extra, to serve

1/2 cup (140g) coconut yogurt (use Home-made Coconut Yogurt on page 21 or buy ready-made)

100g fresh cherries

pancake batter

1 1/4 cups (185g) self-raising flour

2 tbsp Dutch-process cocoa powder

1/2 tsp bicarbonate of soda

1/2 tsp ground cinnamon

3/4 cup (180ml) almond milk

2 tsp apple cider vinegar

1/3 cup (80ml) pure maple syrup

1 Make the pancake batter. Sift the flour, cocoa powder, bicarbonate of soda, and cinnamon into a medium bowl. Whisk together the almond milk, apple cider vinegar, and maple syrup in a small jug. Make a well in the centre of the flour mixture. Gradually pour in the almond milk mixture, whisking continuously, until a smooth batter forms. Allow to stand for 5 minutes.

2 Heat a large non-stick frying pan over a medium heat; brush with a little of the vegetable oil. Working in batches, pour the pancake batter into the pan, using about 1/4 cup (60ml) batter for each pancake. Cook for 2 minutes or until bubbles appear on the surface. Turn the pancakes; cook for a further 1 minute on the other side or until lightly browned. Remove from the pan; cover to keep warm. Repeat with the remaining oil and batter, to make 8 pancakes in total. Reserve the pan.

3 Slice the bananas on a sharp angle. Place the reserved pan over a medium-high heat. Add the maple syrup and bananas to the hot pan; cook for 2 minutes or until caramelized; turn and cook for a further 30 seconds.

4 Serve the pancakes topped with the coconut yogurt, caramelized bananas, cherries, and an extra drizzle of maple syrup.

TIPS

- Dutch-process cocoa powder is treated with an alkalizing ingredient to neutralize cocoa's naturally acidic taste, making it smoother and more mellow.
- Use your favourite berries instead of cherries.
- The pancakes can be frozen for up to 1 month; simply reheat from frozen when needed.

Spiced pecan French toast

PREP + COOK TIME **25 MINUTES** | SERVES **4**

The trick to cooking this toast perfectly is to keep an eye on the heat to ensure that the nuts don't scorch. The result is crisp-coated, spice-infused heaven, and the sweet acidity of the fresh berries provides the ideal counterbalance to the rich flavours and textures.

1¹/₂ cups (375ml) coconut milk

2 tsp vanilla extract

¹/₂ cup (125ml) pure maple syrup

¹/₃ cup (35g) hazelnut meal

1 tbsp nutritional yeast flakes (see tips)

¹/₂ tsp mixed spice

1 cup (120g) pecans, finely chopped

8 thick slices of multigrain sourdough bread

40g vegan margarine spread

250g mixed berries such as strawberries, blueberries, and raspberries

2 tsp vegan icing sugar

unsprayed edible flowers (optional)

1 Whisk together the coconut milk, vanilla, 2 tablespoons of the maple syrup, hazelnut meal, nutritional yeast flakes, and mixed spice in a shallow dish. Put the pecans on a plate, spreading in an even layer. Soak the bread in the coconut milk mixture, a slice at a time, for 1 minute on each side. Press onto the pecans.

2 Heat half of the margarine in a large frying pan over a medium-low heat. Cook the bread, in batches, for 2 minutes on each side or until golden, adding the remaining margarine halfway through cooking.

3 Divide the French toast among 4 serving plates; top with the berries and remaining syrup. Dust with the icing sugar. Serve topped with edible flowers, if you like.

TIPS

• Use ground almonds instead of hazelnut meal, if you like, and olive oil instead of vegan margarine.

• Nutritional yeast is deactivated yeast, having been heat-treated so that it cannot ferment. A complete protein, it contains 18 amino acids, including the nine that are essential for good health. It is generally fortified with vitamin B12, an important nutrient for vegans that is lacking in a meat-free diet. Nutritional yeast is available from health food shops and online.

Fig and orange chia puddings

PREP + COOK TIME **15 MINUTES + STANDING + REFRIGERATION** | SERVES **4**

Figs and chia seeds are sources of dietary fibre and protein, which provide satiety. They are also, along with almonds, non-dairy sources of calcium. Turkish figs are traditionally sun-dried, making them meatier and more aromatic than other dried figs.

You will need to start this recipe at least 2 hours ahead

5 dried Turkish figs (80g)

2 cups (500ml) almond milk

1/2 tsp vanilla bean powder

1 tbsp pure maple syrup

1 tsp finely grated orange zest, plus extra strips of zest, to decorate (optional; see tips)

1/2 cup (80g) white chia seeds, plus extra, to decorate (optional)

1 cup (280g) coconut yogurt (use Home-made Coconut Yogurt on page 21 or buy ready-made)

150g blueberries

150g blackberries

2 small fresh figs (100g), cut into wedges

1/2 cup (75g) cherries

1/4 cup unsprayed edible flowers (optional)

1 Put the dried figs in a small bowl with 1 cup (250ml) water; allow to stand for at least 2 hours. Drain the figs, discarding the liquid.

2 Put the drained figs in a high-powered blender with the almond milk, vanilla bean powder, maple syrup, and orange zest; blend until smooth. Transfer the mixture to a medium bowl; whisk in the chia seeds until evenly combined.

3 Pour the mixture into four 3/4-cup (180ml) glasses, bowls, or dishes. Cover, then refrigerate for at least 2 hours or overnight.

4 Blend the yogurt and half of the blueberries until smooth; spoon the yogurt mixture over the fig mixture, dividing evenly among the glasses.

5 Serve the puddings topped with the blackberries, remaining blueberries, fresh figs, and cherries. Sprinkle with extra strips of orange zest, extra chia seeds, and edible flowers, if you like.

TIPS

• These puddings are best made the night before serving. They will keep for up to 3 days in the fridge.

• To make orange zest to decorate, use a zester to remove the zest from half an orange. (Or, thinly peel the zest from the orange using a vegetable peeler; remove any white pith, then cut the zest into long, thin strips.)

• For a summery dessert, decorate the puddings with heart-shaped vegan chocolates.

Nut and seed butter

PREP + COOK TIME **30 MINUTES** | MAKES **1¹/₂ CUPS**

This delicious non-dairy butter alternative is suitable not only for vegans, but also for those who are lactose-intolerant. The butter is very lightly sweetened, but can still be used as a spread for savoury sandwiches. Simply omit the maple syrup, if you like.

1 cup (160g) blanched almonds, roasted
¹/₂ cup (70g) roasted unsalted peanuts
¹/₂ cup (75g) sunflower seeds
¹/₄ cup (40g) golden linseeds (flaxseeds)
¹/₄ cup (60ml) light-flavoured extra virgin olive oil
1 tbsp pure maple syrup
¹/₂ tsp sea salt flakes

1 Process all the ingredients, scraping the side of the bowl regularly, until the mixture is smooth. Alternatively, use a high-powered blender for a faster and smoother result. (This step may take up to 25 minutes, depending on the processing power of your processor or blender. Powerful commercial processors and blenders will take around 10 minutes, while small retail home-use blenders/processors can take up to 25 minutes before the mixture becomes smooth.)

2 Spoon the nut and seed butter into a jar with a tight-fitting lid; refrigerate. It will keep, refrigerated in an airtight container, for up to 3 weeks. Stir before using, as the oil will settle on the top.

3 Spread the nut and seed butter on your favourite toast or crispbread, then top with fruit such as sliced sweet melon, kiwi fruit, mandarin segments, thinly sliced apple, sliced strawberries, sliced avocado with sesame seeds or edible flowers, sliced banana, or blueberries.

TIPS

- If you like, swap the almonds and peanuts for cashews and macadamias; omit the linseeds, and stir in 2 tablespoons poppy seeds at the end.
- For a chocolatey breakfast spread, add 1¹/₂ tablespoons Dutch-process cocoa powder and an extra 1 tablespoon maple syrup to the ingredients.
- For crunchy nut butter, reserve ¹/₂ cup (about 75g) of the nuts, and pulse through at the end of blending.

Home-made coconut yogurt

PREP + COOK TIME 15 MINUTES + STERILIZATION + STANDING + REFRIGERATION | MAKES 4³/₄ CUPS (ABOUT 1.3KG)

Best enjoyed for breakfast or as a dessert topped with fresh or poached fruit, this coconut milk yogurt is not suitable for cooking. Remember that you will need to start the recipe 2 days ahead, to allow time for fermentation. Also, the yogurt mixture is poured into sterilized jars to set; see the instructions for sterilizing jars below. Don't skip this step – it's important.

You will need to start this recipe 2 days ahead

¹/₄ cup (30g) tapioca flour

800ml canned coconut milk (see tips)

400ml canned coconut cream (see tips)

3 probiotic capsules (see tips)

1 tbsp pure maple syrup

fresh fruit and unsprayed edible flowers, to serve

1 Sterilize the jars (see below).

2 Whisk together the tapioca flour and ¹/₄ cup (60ml) of the coconut milk in a small bowl until smooth and combined.

3 Pour the tapioca mixture into a medium saucepan; whisk in the remaining coconut milk and the coconut cream until combined. Stir the mixture over a low heat for 10 minutes or until it boils and thickens. Remove the pan from the heat. Place a cooking thermometer in the pan, then allow to stand until the mixture cools to 43°C/109°F. Once cooled, open the probiotic capsules; add the powder inside and maple syrup to the yogurt mixture, and stir to combine.

4 Transfer the mixture to the warm sterilized jars; seal immediately. Allow to stand in a warm place for 12 hours or until cultured (the mixture will taste slightly sour) and slightly thickened. Refrigerate for 24 hours or until the coconut yogurt thickens further. The coconut yogurt will keep refrigerated for up to 2 weeks.

5 Serve topped with kiwi fruit, figs, blueberries, raspberries, and edible flowers, or any combination of seasonal fruits you like.

TIPS

- Tapioca flour, also known as tapioca starch, is gluten-free and available from large supermarkets, health food shops, and speciality and Asian grocers, as well as online.
- Buy coconut milk and coconut cream without additives, preservatives, and stabilizers; otherwise the set of the yogurt may be affected.
- Probiotic capsules are readily available from pharmacies and health food shops.
- You can keep this yogurt on hand in the refrigerator, to use as a fresh topping for muesli, porridge, or pancakes, if you like.

sterilizing jars Make sure your glass storage jars have no chips or cracks, and any lids provide an airtight seal. Hygiene is important, so ensure your hands are clean and use clean tea towels when holding or moving the jars. Run the jars and lids through the hot rinse cycle in a dishwasher, or wash them in hot soapy water; rinse well. Stand the clean jars, top-side up, on a tray in a cold oven; heat to 120°C (100°C fan/250°F/Gas ¹/₂), then leave the jars in the oven for 30 minutes.

Bircher muesli

Bircher muesli was created at the turn of the 20th century by a Swiss doctor who espoused eating a diet of 50 per cent raw foods for good health. The options below are variations on traditional Bircher muesli, and all feature the signature softened uncooked grains.

Super seed Bircher

PREP TIME **15 MINUTES + REFRIGERATION** | SERVES **4**

Crumble $\frac{1}{2}$ cup (25g) coconut flakes into a medium bowl. Stir in $\frac{1}{3}$ cup (55g) sunflower seeds, $\frac{1}{3}$ cup (55g) pumpkin seeds, $\frac{1}{4}$ cup (40g) white chia seeds, $\frac{1}{4}$ cup (25g) milled flaxseed, and 1¼ cups (310ml) almond milk. Cover, then refrigerate for at least 1 hour or overnight. Cut 2 green apples (300g) into matchsticks, and thickly slice 200g strawberries. Divide the seed mixture among 4 serving bowls; top with the apple and strawberries. Drizzle with coconut nectar syrup or pure maple syrup to serve.

Make-and-go Bircher

PREP TIME **10 MINUTES** | SERVES **2**

Cut 1 large ripe banana (230g) in half. Place each half in a 2-cup (500ml) glass jar; mash with a fork. Cut 1 large (200g) red dessert apple with the skin on into matchsticks; divide evenly between the jars. Add $\frac{1}{2}$ cup (50g) rolled oats and a pinch of ground cinnamon. Top each jar with 1 tablespoon pumpkin seeds and 2 tablespoons blueberries. Stir $\frac{3}{4}$ cup (185ml) almond and coconut milk into each jar. Seal and go.

Pomegranate and pear Bircher

PREP TIME **15 MINUTES + REFRIGERATION** | SERVES **6**

Combine 2 cups (500ml) almond milk and 1 cup (250ml) pomegranate juice in a medium bowl. Add 1 cup (95g) rolled oats, $\frac{1}{2}$ cup (40g) quinoa flakes, and 2 tablespoons white chia seeds; stir to combine. Grate 1 large pear (330g); add to the oat mixture. Stir to combine. Cover, then refrigerate for 3 hours or overnight. Divide the oats among 6 serving bowls, drizzle with pure maple syrup. Top each serving with 1 tablespoon pomegranate seeds, 2 slices of pear, and a little grated orange zest.

Coconut tropical Bircher

PREP TIME **15 MINUTES** | SERVES **4**

Combine 3 cups (240g) quinoa flakes, 1 cup (250ml) coconut milk, 1 cup (250ml) coconut water, and 1 cup (250ml) cloudy apple juice in a medium bowl. Divide the quinoa mixture evenly among 4 serving bowls. Cut 1 small dragon fruit (250g) and 1 small mango (300g) into slices; divide the fruit evenly among the bowls. Serve the Bircher topped with the pulp of 1 passionfruit and ¼ cup (15g) coconut flakes.

TIP

Pomegranate seeds (arils) are sold in small punnets in the fresh food section at supermarkets.

Crunch bowl with berry coconut yogurt

PREP + COOK TIME **40 MINUTES** | SERVES **6**

Seeds are a good source of protein, fibre, and minerals, and pumpkin seeds contain a surprising amount of iron for their size. Inca berries – also known as cape gooseberries or golden berries – are native to South America and have a wonderful tangy flavour.

1 cup (160g) brazil nuts

1/2 cup (80g) natural almonds

1/3 cup (65g) pumpkin seeds

1/3 cup (50g) sunflower seeds

2/3 cup (30g) unsweetened flaked coconut

1/4 cup (35g) cacao nibs

2/3 cup (110g) Inca berries

3 cups (840g) berry coconut yogurt

fresh fruit and unsprayed edible flowers, to serve (see tips)

1 Preheat the oven to 180°C (160°C fan/350°F/Gas 4).

2 Spread the brazil nuts and almonds in an even layer on a baking tray; roast for 10 minutes or until lightly browned and fragrant. Coarsely chop the brazil nuts and almonds; place in a large bowl. Roast the seeds on the baking tray for 8 minutes or until lightly browned; add to the bowl. Roast the coconut on the baking tray for 4 minutes or until lightly browned and fragrant. Add to the bowl with the cacao nibs and Inca berries; stir through to mix evenly.

3 Spoon the crunch bowl mixture into 6 serving bowls, followed by the yogurt. Serve topped with fresh fruit and edible flowers.

TIPS

- Any combination of nuts and seeds can be used in this recipe, or choose your favourite flavour of coconut yogurt instead of berry, if you like.
- Dried Inca berries are high in vitamins C, B, and A, and are available at some supermarkets, health food shops, and online.
- Serve the crunch bowl topped with dragon fruit, honeydew melon, figs, kiwi fruit, cherries, blueberries, strawberries, pomegranate seeds, and raspberries (as in the photograph here). Or use any combination of seasonal fruits you like, adjusting the makeup according to the time of year.
- Make the most of this versatile crunch bowl mix. Serve as a muesli, or sprinkle on top of yogurt or fruit, scattered with unsprayed edible flowers and vegan chocolate, if you like. It also doubles as a trail mix for an energy-rich snack on the go.

Cherry tomato and moxarella bruschetta

PREP + COOK TIME **40 MINUTES + SOAKING + COOLING + REFRIGERATION** | SERVES **4**

If you have it, day-old bread is ideal for bruschetta. The bread will be revived by the gorgeous tomato juices and still retain its texture. To turn this into lunch or a light supper, serve with a side salad topped with sunflower seeds.

You will need to start the vegan mozzarella recipe at least 4 hours ahead

400g vine tomato medley mix

250g cherry vine tomatoes

1 tbsp fresh rosemary or oregano leaves

4 garlic cloves, bruised, halved

2 tbsp extra virgin olive oil

2 tbsp sticky fig and balsamic drizzle (see tips)

8 thick slices of soy and linseed sourdough bread

$2/3$ cup (150g) vegan mozzarella (see right or buy ready-made)

salt and freshly ground black pepper

rocket and walnut pesto

100g rocket, coarsely chopped

$1/2$ cup (80g) toasted walnuts, coarsely chopped

2 tbsp nutritional yeast flakes

$1/2$ cup (125ml) extra virgin olive oil

TIPS

• Use another type of balsamic glaze or reduction, or traditional aged balsamic vinegar, if you like.

• You can buy ready-made mozzarella-style vegan cheese instead of making your own, or swap for vegan cream cheese instead (as pictured here).

• Use vegan mozzarella as a substitute on pizzas or for toasted sandwiches or oven bakes. It will keep in a covered container in the fridge for up to 1 week.

1 To make the rocket and walnut pesto, process the ingredients in a small food processor until almost smooth. Transfer to a small bowl; season with salt and pepper to taste. Set aside until needed.

2 When ready to make the bruschetta, preheat the oven to 180°C (160°C fan/350°F/Gas 4).

3 Arrange the tomatoes, rosemary, and garlic on a medium baking tray. Drizzle with the olive oil and balsamic drizzle; season well with salt and pepper. Roast for 20 minutes. Allow to cool for 5 minutes. Lightly crush the tomatoes; reserve the cooking juices on the tray.

4 Meanwhile, toast the sourdough slices.

5 Top each toast with some of the mozzarella, followed by the tomato mixture. Drizzle with the reserved cooking juices from the tray and the rocket and walnut pesto.

vegan mozzarella Put $1/2$ cup (75g) raw cashews in a small bowl; cover with 3 cups (750ml) cold water. Allow to stand, covered, for 4 hours or overnight. Drain the cashews, then rinse under cold water; drain well. Put in a high-powered blender with $1/2$ cup (70g) macadamias, $2/3$ cup (100g) arrowroot powder, $1/4$ cup (60ml) light-flavoured extra virgin olive oil, $1/4$ cup (25g) nutritional yeast flakes, 2 teaspoons sea salt flakes, and 2 tablespoons lemon juice. Blend until smooth. Pour the mixture into a medium saucepan. Cook, stirring, over a medium heat for 9 minutes or until the mixture becomes very thick and stretchy like melted pizza cheese. Pour the mixture into a 3-cup (750ml) container; allow to cool. Cover with the lid; refrigerate until needed. The mozzarella, which is spreadable, will keep in an airtight container in the fridge for up to 1 week.

Buckini and berry muesli clusters

PREP + COOK TIME **25 MINUTES + COOLING** | MAKES **ABOUT 5 CUPS (550G)**

This toasted muesli is streets ahead of shop-bought versions. Serve the clusters with nut, oat, or soy milk and vegan coconut yogurt (see Home-made Coconut Yogurt on page 21), or alternatively sprinkle over stone fruit or berries as a crunchy topping.

1 cup (110g) rolled oats

1 tsp ground allspice

1/2 tsp ground cardamom

1/2 tsp sea salt flakes

2 tbsp rice malt syrup (see tips)

1 tbsp coconut oil, melted

1 cup (180g) activated buckinis (see tips)

1 cup (30g) puffed quinoa

1 cup (30g) puffed buckwheat

1/4 cup (30g) goji berries

1/4 cup (35g) dried cranberries

1/4 cup (40g) chia seeds

3/4 cup (75g) freeze-dried pomegranate seeds

1 Preheat the oven to 180°C (160°C fan/350°F/Gas 4).

2 Spread the oats in an even layer on a large shallow-sided baking tray. Sprinkle with the spices and salt, then drizzle with the rice malt syrup and coconut oil; toss to coat. Bake for 10 minutes or until the mixture is sticky and golden, stirring once during the cooking time. Allow to cool, then break into clusters. Use a spatula to scrape the mixture from the tray, as it will be caramelized.

3 Put the remaining ingredients in a large bowl with the oat clusters; toss to combine. Store in a glass jar with a tight-fitting lid or a similar airtight container. The muesli will keep at room temperature for up to 2 months.

TIPS

▪ If you can't find rice malt syrup, you can substitute barley malt syrup or agave syrup instead.

▪ Buckinis, also known as activated buckwheat, are gluten-free and high in protein. They are available in some health food shops. You can replace with puffed quinoa or buckwheat with puffed rice, if you like.

▪ Any dried fruit works well here. Try to buy sulphate-free dried fruit that has no added sugar. Freeze-dried pomegranate seeds are available from some supermarkets and health food shops.

▪ To make your own muesli bars, heat some rice malt syrup until bubbling and beginning to caramelize; toss through the muesli. Press into a rectangular or square shallow cake tin lined with baking parchment. Allow to cool, then cut into bars.

Baked porridge with stone fruit

PREP + COOK TIME **55 MINUTES** | SERVES **6**

While baked porridge takes longer to cook than the usual stovetop method, it is still convenient because it cooks without stirring or tending, and rewards with a delicious creaminess. Serve with a dollop of the Home-made Coconut Yogurt on page 21, if you like.

1½ cups (135g) rolled oats

½ cup (40g) desiccated coconut

½ tsp ground cinnamon

½ tsp ground ginger

pinch of sea salt

¼ cup (90g) pure maple syrup

1 tsp vanilla extract

3 cups (750ml) rice milk

2 rhubarb stems (125g), trimmed, cut into 4cm lengths

3 plums (350g), halved

2 nectarines or peaches (340g), cut into thick wedges

2 tbsp coconut sugar

unsprayed edible flowers, to serve (optional)

1 Preheat the oven to 180°C (160°C fan/350°F/Gas 4). Grease a 1.25-litre (5-cup) ovenproof dish.

2 Combine the rolled oats, coconut, cinnamon, ginger, sea salt, maple syrup, and vanilla extract in an ovenproof dish; stir in the rice milk.

3 Bake for 40 minutes or until the oats are tender and creamy.

4 Meanwhile, put the rhubarb and stone fruit in a small baking dish. Sprinkle with the coconut sugar and ⅓ cup (80ml) water. Bake with the porridge, on a separate shelf, for the last 20 minutes of the porridge cooking time.

5 Serve the porridge topped with the baked stone fruit, fruit syrup, and edible flowers, if you like.

TIPS

- You can use soy, almond, or coconut milk in place of the rice milk, if you like.
- In winter, try roast pears and rhubarb instead of nectarines or peaches. Firm pears may take a little longer to cook, so don't forget to factor this in.

Chickpea pancakes with spicy baked beans

PREP + COOK TIME **30 MINUTES** | SERVES **4**

Chickpea flour has a wonderful nutty taste and a naturally higher protein content than wheat-based flours; it is also gluten-free. The trick when adding the water to the flour for the pancake batter is to ensure that the water is cool from the tap, not hot.

1 cup (260g) hummus

2 canned chipotle chillies in adobo sauce

2 cups (300g) chickpea flour (besan or gram flour)

1 tsp baking powder

1 tsp garlic powder

¼ cup (60ml) extra virgin olive oil

80g kale leaves, thinly sliced

2 x 420g cans baked beans

1 tbsp Mexican-style spice mix or chilli powder

2 avocados (500g)

4 radishes (140g), trimmed

½ cup (15g) loosely packed coriander sprigs

salt and freshly ground black pepper

1 lime, cut into wedges, to serve

1 Blend or process the hummus and chipotle chillies until combined. Set aside until needed.

2 Whisk together the chickpea flour, baking powder, and garlic powder in a medium bowl until well combined. Make a well in the centre. Add 2 cups (500ml) water; whisk until the mixture forms a batter. Season with salt and pepper to taste.

3 Heat 1 tablespoon of the olive oil in a large non-stick frying pan over a medium heat; cook the kale, stirring, for 2 minutes or until wilted. Remove from the pan; cover to keep warm.

4 Heat another 2 teaspoons of the olive oil in the same pan. Add a quarter of the pancake mixture; cook for 2 minutes on each side or until light golden. Transfer to a plate; cover to keep warm. Repeat with the remaining olive oil and pancake batter to make 4 pancakes in total.

5 Meanwhile, stir the baked beans and spice mix in a small saucepan over a low heat until hot. Thinly slice the avocados and radishes, to have ready with the other pancake toppings.

6 Serve the pancakes topped with the hummus mixture, baked beans, avocado, wilted kale, radishes, coriander, and lime wedges for squeezing over the top.

TIPS

▪ The pancakes are best made on the day of serving.
▪ You can use spinach, baby spinach, or Swiss chard in place of the kale, if you like.
▪ The baked beans can be heated in the microwave.

Pea and edamame toasts with avocado and umeboshi

PREP + COOK TIME **25 MINUTES** | MAKES **4**

Umeboshi, or Japanese pickled plums, have an intense salty-sour flavour and are used as a condiment in Japanese cuisine. They also have a long history of use as a traditional remedy and are believed to reduce fatigue, stimulate digestion, and eliminate toxins.

1 cup (100g) frozen edamame pods

1 cup (120g) frozen garden peas

1/2 cup (10g) loosely packed mint leaves

1 tbsp lemon juice

2 tbsp extra virgin olive oil, plus extra 2 tbsp for brushing and drizzling

4 slices of sourdough bread, toasted

1 tbsp umeboshi paste (see tips)

1 small avocado (200g), sliced

2 watermelon radishes (70g), trimmed, thinly sliced

1 tbsp micro herbs

salt and freshly ground black pepper

1 Add the edamame to a medium saucepan of boiling water; cook for 2 minutes. Add the frozen peas; cook for a further 2 minutes or until tender. Drain; rinse under cold water to refresh and stop the cooking process. Shell the edamame; discard the pods.

2 Process the edamame, peas, and mint until combined but still chunky. Add the lemon juice and a little of the 2 tablespoons olive oil. With the motor operating, gradually add the remaining olive oil in a thin stream until the mixture is a spreadable consistency. Transfer to a small bowl; season with salt and pepper to taste.

3 Brush each slice of bread with a little of the extra 2 tablespoons olive oil. Toast the bread on a heated grill plate or in a ridged cast-iron grill pan over a high heat until browned on both sides.

4 Spread the sourdough toast with the umeboshi paste and pea mixture. Top with the avocado, radishes, and micro herbs. Season with salt and pepper to taste. Drizzle with a little more olive oil, if you like.

TIPS

▪ Umeboshi paste, made from fermented Japanese ume plums, is available from Japanese grocers and some health food shops. If you can't find it, use seasoned Japanese plum (shiraboshi-ume) instead. Remove the skin and seed; mash the pulp.
▪ The pea mixture can be made several hours ahead. Prepare from step 3 just before serving.

Peanut butter and maple syrup crunch

PREP + COOK TIME **1 HOUR + COOLING** | MAKES **4 CUPS (ABOUT 600G)**

Golden linseeds (flaxseeds) are a rich source of heart-healthy omega-3 fatty acids and may help in the prevention of some cancers. Serve the crunch topped with coconut yogurt, apple, raspberries, nut, or soy milk, then drizzled with extra maple syrup, if you like.

$1/3$ cup (95g) smooth natural peanut butter

$1/4$ cup (50g) coconut oil

$1/4$ cup (90g) pure maple syrup

1 tsp vanilla bean paste

$1^1/2$ cups (135g) rolled oats

$1^1/2$ cups (150g) rolled barley

$1/4$ cup (50g) amaranth grain (see tips)

$1/3$ cup (65g) pumpkin seeds

2 tbsp golden linseeds (flaxseeds)

$1/3$ cup (45g) chopped roasted salted peanuts

1 Preheat the oven to 160°C (140°C fan/325°F/Gas 3). Line 2 baking trays with baking parchment.

2 Stir together the peanut butter, coconut oil, maple syrup, and vanilla bean paste in a small saucepan over a low heat until melted and smooth.

3 Combine the rolled oats, rolled barley, and amaranth in a large bowl. Pour in the peanut butter mixture; stir until combined. Spread over each of the lined trays in an even layer.

4 Bake for 20 minutes, stirring once. Stir in the pumpkin seeds and golden linseeds; bake for a further 30 minutes, stirring every 10 minutes, or until golden. Stir in the peanuts; allow to cool on the trays. Store in an airtight container until needed.

TIPS

- An ancient grain, amaranth is a pseudocereal similar to quinoa and buckwheat. Gluten-free and a good source of fibre and essential vitamins and minerals, the seeds can be toasted, baked, ground into flour, or used in a porridge, but must always be cooked before eating.
- Replace the rolled barley with extra rolled oats, if you like. Amaranth can be replaced with chia seeds.
- The crunch will keep in an airtight glass jar or container for up to 1 month.

Spinach and tomato 'omelette'

PREP + COOK TIME **20 MINUTES** | MAKES **2**

Making your own nut-based marinated vegan feta is easy, and it's a great stand-by to have
in the fridge. Simply follow the recipe below so that you have it on hand when you need it.
The longer you allow the feta to marinate, the stronger the flavours will be.

**You will need to start the marinated feta
at least 1 day ahead if making your own**

300g silken tofu

2 tbsp extra virgin olive oil

1/3 cup (80ml) soy milk

1/3 cup (50g) chickpea flour (besan or gram flour)

2 tbsp nutritional yeast flakes

1/2 tsp sea salt flakes

1/4 tsp ground turmeric

spinach filling

120g fresh spinach leaves

1 shallot, thinly sliced

200g heirloom cherry tomatoes,
sliced or halved

1 tbsp red wine vinegar

2 tbsp extra virgin olive oil

60g drained marinated vegan feta (see tip)

1 To make the 'omelette' mixture, pat the tofu dry with kitchen paper.
Blend the tofu with 1 tablespoon of the olive oil and the remaining
ingredients in a blender until smooth.

2 Heat a 22cm non-stick frying pan over a high heat. Add 2 teaspoons
of the olive oil; reduce the heat to medium-high. Add half of the tofu
mixture; swirl or spread the mixture until the bottom of the pan is
covered. Cook for 3 minutes or until small bubbles appear on the surface.
Slide the omelette onto a warm plate; cover to keep warm. Repeat with
the remaining olive oil and tofu mixture to make a second omelette;
slide onto a second warm plate.

3 Make the spinach filling. Put the spinach leaves, shallot, tomatoes, red
wine vinegar, and olive oil in a medium bowl; toss gently to combine.
Top with the vegan feta.

4 Divide the filling between the omelettes, placing it over half of each
omelette; fold over the omelettes to cover the filling. Serve immediately.

marinated vegan feta Put 3/4 cup (115g) raw cashews and 3/4 cup (105g) raw
macadamias in a bowl with enough water to cover; allow to stand for 8 hours or
overnight. Drain the nuts; rinse well. Process the nuts with 1 tablespoon nutritional
yeast flakes, 1 teaspoon sea salt flakes, 1/4 cup (60ml) lemon juice, and 1/4 cup
(60ml) extra virgin olive oil until smooth. Press the mixture firmly into a
cling-film-lined 9cm x 15cm container. Turn out onto a baking tray lined with
baking parchment. Preheat the oven to 200°C (180°C fan/400°F/Gas 6). Bake the
mixture for 20 minutes or until golden. Allow to cool, then cut into squares. Store
in a glass jar or similar, covered in olive oil, with sprigs of fresh rosemary and
thyme, and peeled garlic cloves. The marinated feta will keep in the fridge for
up to 2 weeks. (Makes about 220g)

TIP

There are various ready-made feta-style vegan
cheeses available for you to choose from, if you don't
want to make your own. You could also use other
styles of vegan cheese or crumbled tofu or tempeh.

Avocado toasts with smoky chickpeas

PREP + COOK TIME **15 MINUTES** | SERVES **2**

Simple to put together but brimming with flavour, this easy breakfast will kick-start your day with good portions of protein, fibre, and healthy fats. Chickpeas and avocado are nutrient-rich, providing essential vitamins and minerals such as manganese, folate, and potassium.

1 cup (190g) drained canned chickpeas, rinsed (see tips)

2 tbsp extra virgin olive oil

1/2 tsp sea salt flakes

1/2 tsp smoked paprika

1/2 tsp ground cumin

4 slices of wholegrain sourdough bread, toasted

1 large avocado (320g), mashed

1/3 cup (15g) micro herbs (see tips)

2 tbsp sriracha

lime wedges, to serve

1 Pat the chickpeas dry with kitchen paper. Heat the olive oil in a large frying pan over a high heat. Add the chickpeas and salt; cook, stirring occasionally, for 5 minutes. Add the smoked paprika and cumin; cook, stirring, for a further 30 seconds.

2 Spread the sourdough toast with the mashed avocado. Top with the smoky chickpeas and micro herbs; drizzle with the sriracha. Serve with lime wedges for squeezing over.

TIPS

• The drained liquid from the chickpeas, called aquafaba, can be used to make vegan meringue (see Frozen No-Bake Blueberry and Lime Meringue Slab on page 158). Aquafaba can be stored in a container in the fridge for 2 days or frozen for up to 3 months.

• You can use micro parsley or coriander, or any full-sized chopped soft-leaf herb such as flat-leaf parsley, dill, coriander, or mint.

Maple butternut waffles with pecans

PREP + COOK TIME **1 HOUR + STANDING** | SERVES **4**

This vegan waffle recipe is a jaw-dropping way to start (or end) your day. With the sweetness of squash and maple syrup, and the buttery toastiness of pecans, it's a dream come true. Butternut is the best variety of winter squash to use here, as it has dry, dense flesh.

1^1/$_3$ cups (200g) white spelt flour

2 tsp baking powder

^{1}/$_2$ tsp sea salt flakes

2 tsp mixed spice

^{3}/$_4$ cup (180ml) almond milk

^{1}/$_4$ cup (60ml) olive oil

^{1}/$_2$ cup (120g) mashed cooked butternut squash (see tip)

2 tbsp pure maple syrup, plus extra, to serve

2 tsp vanilla extract

cooking oil spray

4 scoops of dairy-free vanilla ice cream

^{2}/$_3$ cup (80g) coarsely chopped pecans, roasted

1 Sift together the flour, baking powder, salt, and mixed spice in a large bowl. In a separate bowl, combine the almond milk, olive oil, mashed butternut squash, the 2 tablespoons maple syrup, and vanilla until smooth.

2 Pour the squash mixture into the flour mixture; stir until just combined but still with some lumps. Allow the batter to stand for 10 minutes.

3 Preheat the waffle iron according to the manufacturer's instructions; spray with a little cooking oil.

4 Gently stir the batter. Pour ¼ cup (60ml) of the batter onto the centre of each square section of the waffle iron to just cover the bottom. Close the lid; cook for 3 minutes or until golden brown. Transfer to a wire rack. Repeat with the remaining batter to make a total of 8 waffles.

5 Serve the waffles topped with the scoops of ice cream, chopped pecans, and extra maple syrup.

TIP

For mashed squash, cook 180g peeled, seeded, chopped butternut squash with 1 tablespoon water, in a microwave-safe bowl covered with plastic wrap, on HIGH (100%) for 8 minutes or until tender; mash. Alternatively, steam the squash in a steamer over a saucepan of simmering water until tender; mash.

Crushed pea and pickled vegetable toasts

PREP + COOK TIME **15 MINUTES** | SERVES **4**

Pickled vegetables such as kimchi and sauerkraut are traditionally preserved using lactic acid fermentation. Eating fermented foods adds live microbes to the existing colony of microbes that live in our gut, contributing to good and balanced health.

3 cups (360g) frozen garden peas

1/3 cup (90g) hulled tahini

2 tbsp fresh dill leaves

1 garlic clove, crushed

2 tbsp lemon juice

1 tbsp Dijon mustard

2 tbsp sunflower seeds

2 tsp sesame seeds

2 tsp linseeds (flaxseeds)

8 slices of sprouted bread (see tips)

1 1/3 cups (240g) drained shop-bought fermented vegetables of choice

1 cup (15g) loosely packed mangetout tendrils or other pea shoots

salt and freshly ground black pepper

1/2 lemon, cut into 4 wedges

1   Put the peas in a heatproof bowl; cover with boiling water. Allow to stand for 2 minutes; drain. Blend or process the peas, tahini, dill, garlic, lemon juice, and Dijon mustard until a chunky spread forms. Season with salt and pepper to taste.

2   Put the sunflower seeds, sesame seeds, and linseeds in a small heavy-based frying pan. Toast the seeds over a medium-high heat, stirring constantly, until lightly browned.

3   Top the toasted bread with the pea spread, fermented vegetables, toasted seeds, and pea shoots. Serve with the lemon wedges for squeezing over.

TIPS

• Good-quality sprouted-grain bread is available from some health food shops, artesan bakers, and gourmet grocers and markets; keep refrigerated.

• The pea spread can be kept in an airtight container in the fridge for up to 1 day. Toast the bread and assemble the toasts just before serving.

Almond milk and mango pikelets

PREP + COOK TIME **25 MINUTES + STANDING** | SERVES **4**

This is nothing fancy – just an honest-to-goodness sweet fix to whip up in minutes because sometimes that's all you want. You can choose a different seasonal fruit, if you like, or turn this into a dessert by topping the pikelets with scoops of dairy-free vanilla ice cream.

1½ cups (225g) self-raising flour

1 tsp baking powder

1 tbsp golden caster sugar

1½ cups (375ml) almond milk

1 tbsp coconut oil, melted

½ tsp vanilla extract

¼ cup (55g) firmly packed soft brown sugar

2 small mangoes (600g), sliced

⅓ cup (25g) natural flaked almonds, toasted (optional; see tip)

1 Sift the flour, baking powder, and caster sugar into a medium bowl. Gradually whisk in the almond milk, coconut oil, and vanilla extract until smooth. Allow to stand for 15 minutes.

2 Heat a large non-stick frying pan over a medium heat. Using 2 tablespoons of batter for each pikelet, cook about 4 pikelets at a time for 2 minutes or until bubbles appear on the surface. Turn; cook on the other side until golden. Remove the pikelets from the pan; cover to keep warm. Repeat with the remaining batter, to make 12 pikelets in total.

3 Heat ½ cup (125ml) water and the brown sugar in a medium frying pan over a low heat, stirring, until the sugar has dissolved. Bring to the boil. Boil, uncovered, for 3 minutes or until the syrup thickens slightly.

4 Serve the warm pikelets with the mango, syrup, and toasted almonds, if you like.

TIP

Toasting nuts brings out the flavour. There are two ways to toast them: Spread the nuts onto a baking tray, roast in a 180°C (160°C fan/350°F/Gas 4) oven for 5–10 minutes until the nuts are golden brown (stir once during roasting for even cooking). Or, put the nuts in a heavy-based frying pan; stir continuously over a medium heat until evenly browned.

PACK
AND GO

Appetizing snacks, appealing lunches,
nutritious, quick-to-put-together options for
hectic lifestyles – and all ideal for eating at
home or taking with you when on the go.

Cauliflower dip with rice crackers

PREP + COOK TIME **1 HOUR 30 MINUTES + SOAKING** | SERVES **4 (MAKES 3 CUPS)**

Roasting cauliflower allows it to caramelize, bringing out its earthy flavour and natural sweetness – particularly when it is paired with earthy spice mixes such as dukkah. Serve with crudités such as sliced cucumber, radishes, and baby carrots.

400g cauliflower, cut into florets

1/4 cup (60ml) extra virgin olive oil

2 tbsp hazelnut dukkah

3 garlic cloves, unpeeled

1/2 cup (140g) dairy-free yogurt

400g canned cannellini beans, drained, rinsed

2 tbsp lemon juice

1/4 cup (35g) coarsely chopped roasted hazelnuts

salt and freshly ground black pepper

rice crackers

1/4 cup (45g) linseeds (flaxseeds)

1/3 cup (70g) red quinoa, rinsed

1 cup (175g) cooked brown rice (see tips)

1 tsp sea salt

2 tsp tamari

1 1/2 tbsp extra virgin olive oil

1/3 cup (50g) sesame seeds, toasted

TIPS

- The crackers can be made a week ahead. Store in an airtight container until needed.
- You can use precooked brown rice for this recipe, or boil about 1/3 cup (65g) uncooked brown rice.

1   First, make the rice crackers. Put the linseeds in a small bowl; add enough water to cover. Allow to stand for at least 20 minutes. Drain well, then pat dry with kitchen paper.

2   Meanwhile, put the quinoa and 2 cups (500ml) water in a small saucepan; bring to the boil. Simmer, uncovered, for 12 minutes or until tender. Drain well; allow to cool.

3   Blend or process the linseeds, quinoa, rice, sea salt, tamari, and olive oil in a food processor until the mixture forms a ball; add 1 tablespoon water, if needed, to bring it together. Add the sesame seeds; pulse to combine. The dough will be very sticky.

4   Preheat the oven to 200°C (180°C fan/400°F/Gas 6). Divide the dough in half. Roll each half between sheets of baking parchment until 2mm thick. Remove the top layer of baking parchment. Using a knife, score the top of the dough into desired shapes; slide, still on the parchment, onto baking trays. Bake for 40 minutes or until crisp and golden. Allow to cool for 5 minutes; break the crackers along the score lines. Cool completely.

5   To make the cauliflower dip, preheat the oven to 220°C (200°C fan/425°F/ Gas 7). Line a baking tray with baking parchment.

6   Place the cauliflower on the prepared tray. Drizzle with half of the olive oil; sprinkle with 1 tablespoon of the dukkah. Toss to coat. Add the garlic to the same tray. Roast for 30 minutes or until tender. Allow to cool to room temperature.

7   Process the cauliflower, peeled garlic, yogurt, cannellini beans, lemon juice, and remaining olive oil until smooth. Season with salt and pepper to taste. Transfer to a serving bowl. Sprinkle with the hazelnuts and the remaining 1 tablespoon dukkah.

8   Serve the dip with the crackers and crudités, if you like. Season with salt and pepper to taste.

Sweet potato, black bean, and feta sausage rolls

PREP + COOK TIME **1 HOUR 5 MINUTES** | MAKES **12**

A meat-free variation on a family favourite, these sausage rolls pack a flavour punch. With good carbohydrates, fibre, and protein from the sweet potato and black beans, they are both nutritious and filling. Great straight from the oven, they also make an ideal portable lunch.

750g orange sweet potatoes, peeled, cut into 2cm cubes

1 red onion (170g), finely chopped

olive oil cooking spray

400g can black beans, drained, rinsed

1/3 cup (20g) coarsely chopped flat-leaf parsley

1/4 cup (40g) pine nuts, toasted, coarsely chopped

100g marinated or herbed vegan feta, crumbled (see tips)

2 sheets of frozen vegan puff pastry (330g), just thawed

1 tbsp soy milk

2 tsp black sesame seeds

2 tsp white sesame seeds

1 cup (320g) tomato relish

salt and freshly ground black pepper

1 Preheat the oven to 180°C (160°C fan/350°F/Gas 4). Line 2 oven trays with baking parchment.

2 Place the sweet potato and onion on one of the trays. Lightly spray with olive oil; season with salt and pepper to taste. Roast for 30 minutes or until the sweet potato is soft. Allow to cool slightly. Increase the oven temperature to 230°C (210°C fan/450°F/Gas 8).

3 Put the roasted sweet potatoes and onion in a large bowl with the black beans; lightly crush using a fork. Add the parsley and pine nuts; mix well. Gently fold in the feta.

4 Cut the puff pastry sheets in half. Place a quarter of the filling mixture along one long edge; brush the opposite edge with a little of the soy milk. Roll up to enclose the filling. Cut the roll into 3 pieces; place, seam-side down, on the second lined tray. Repeat with the remaining pastry and filling mixture to make 12 sausage rolls.

5 Brush the tops of the rolls with the remaining soy milk; sprinkle with the combined sesame seeds.

6 Bake the sausage rolls for 30 minutes or until golden brown. Serve hot or at room temperature, accompanied by the relish.

TIPS

- You can make the marinated vegan feta on page 38 and use it in this recipe instead of buying it.
- Use spiced tofu instead of vegan feta, if you like.
- If you don't have relish on hand, replace with tomato ketchup or your favourite chutney instead.

Tofu banh mi rolls

PREP + COOK TIME **15 MINUTES** | MAKES **2**

Vietnamese banh mi rolls are a popular street food often eaten for breakfast or as a snack. Fillings vary, but all reflect the fusion of Vietnamese ingredients with French-style baguettes and condiments such as mayonnaise. Use crusty, baguette-like bread rolls for best results.

150g undressed coleslaw salad mix (see tips)

1/4 cup (7g) fresh coriander leaves

1/4 cup (75g) vegan mayonnaise (use the recipe for Everyday Mayo at right or buy ready-made)

2 tsp rice wine vinegar

1/2 tsp sesame oil

1/2 tsp sea salt flakes

1 tsp olive oil

200g satay marinated tofu (see tips)

2 crusty bread rolls such as ficelles (mini baguettes)

1 Put the coleslaw salad mix and coriander in a medium bowl. Add 1 tablespoon of the vegan mayonnaise, the rice wine vinegar, sesame oil, and sea salt; toss to coat well.

2 Heat the olive oil in a medium frying pan over a medium-high heat; cook the marinated tofu for 2 minutes on each side or until golden and heated through.

3 Split the bread rolls in half lengthways; spread both sides with the remaining mayonnaise. Fill with the fried tofu and coleslaw mixture.

everyday mayo Drain all liquid (aquafaba) from a 400g can of chickpeas; you will need 1/4 cup (60ml) aquafaba. Blend the reserved aquafaba with 1 tablespoon apple cider vinegar, 1/2 teaspoon sea salt flakes, and 1/2 teaspoon Dijon mustard in a small blender (do not use a food processor) until smooth. With the motor operating, add 1/2 cup (125ml) olive oil in a slow, steady stream until thick and creamy (the mayonnaise will thicken further in the fridge). Spoon the mayonnaise into a screw-top jar with a tight-fitting lid. Store in the fridge for up to 2 weeks. (Makes 2 cups/500ml)

chilli mayonnaise Make the Everyday Mayo as above. Stir in 1 teaspoon smoked paprika, 2 teaspoons tomato purée, 1 crushed garlic clove, and 1/4 teaspoon chilli flakes. Serve with the vegan burgers on page 132 or anything to which you'd like to add a little kick of smoky chilli flavour.

turmeric mayonnaise First make the Everyday Mayo. Stir in 1/2 teaspoon ground turmeric, 2 tablespoons finely grated carrot, 2 tablespoons white miso paste (shiro miso), and 1 tablespoon sesame oil. This mayonnaise works well with most things.

TIPS

• Make your own coleslaw mix if you cannot find undressed coleslaw, using a combination of red and white cabbage, carrot, and even beetroot, if you like.

• You can use your favourite Asian-style marinated tofu instead of satay-flavoured tofu.

• To make your own satay marinated tofu, combine 1 cup (260g) crunchy peanut butter, 1 tablespoon kecap manis (sweet soy sauce), and 2 teaspoons groundnut oil with 200g firm tofu; refrigerate for 20 minutes before cooking.

Beetroot monster munch balls

PREP + COOK TIME **20 MINUTES + REFRIGERATION** | MAKES **28**

These protein balls are a perfect snack on the go, or can be served for morning or afternoon tea with herbal tea or freshly squeezed juice. As an energy-rich treat, they also make a great pre- or post-workout snack.

1 cup (160g) natural almonds

1 cup (140g) dried dates, pitted

2 large beetroot (400g), trimmed and peeled, finely grated

1/2 cup (60g) goji berries

1/4 cup (40g) chia seeds

1/4 cup (25g) cacao powder

1/4 cup (35g) lucuma powder (see tips)

1 tbsp psyllium husks

1/2 cup (80g) activated buckinis

1/4 cup (90g) rice malt syrup

freeze-dried raspberries (optional)

1 Process the almonds and dates until a slightly coarse crumb forms; transfer to a large bowl. Add the remaining ingredients, except for the raspberries; mix well with your hands until combined. (Use disposable gloves to protect your hands from staining from the beetroot, if you like.)

2 Roll 1 tablespoon of the mixture into a ball; roll in the crushed freeze-dried raspberries, if using. You will need to press the raspberry coating into the side of the ball slightly, to help it stick. Place the coated ball on a tray; repeat with the remaining mixture.

3 Cover the protein balls on the tray, then refrigerate for 4 hours or until firm. Transfer to an airtight container.

TIPS

- Lucuma powder, ground from a Peruvian fruit, has a creamy, citrus flavour. It's available from some health food shops or can be ordered online.
- Roll the protein balls in chopped nuts such as pistachios, sifted cacao powder, goji berries, or toasted shredded coconut instead of the freeze-dried raspberries, if you like.
- These protein balls will keep in an airtight container for up to 1 week in the fridge or can be frozen for up to 2 months; they can be eaten straight from the freezer.

Mexican quinoa pots

PREP + COOK TIME **35 MINUTES** | SERVES **2**

Make the pots with white, red, or tri-coloured quinoa, or use other whole grains such as
barley or farro. Assembling the salad in jars makes it simple to transport for lunch at work,
for instance, but you can use any container you like for ease and convenience.

$1/2$ cup (100g) white quinoa, rinsed

1 sweetcorn cob (400g), husks and silks removed

400g can black beans, drained, rinsed

1 small red pepper (150g), finely chopped

2 spring onions, thinly sliced

$1^1/2$ tbsp extra virgin olive oil

2 tbsp lime juice

1 fresh long red chilli, thinly sliced

1 small avocado (200g)

1 small garlic clove, crushed

2 sprigs of coriander

2 lime wedges

salt and freshly ground black pepper

tortilla chips, to serve (optional)

1 Put the quinoa and 2 cups (500ml) water in a small saucepan over a
medium-high heat; bring to the boil. Reduce the heat to low; simmer
for 12 minutes or until tender. Drain; rinse under cold water.

2 Heat a ridged cast-iron grill pan (or heavy-based frying pan) over a high
heat. Cook the sweetcorn cob, rotating so that it cooks all over, for
12 minutes or until lightly charred. Allow to cool slightly, then cut the
kernels from the cob using a sharp knife.

3 Put the cooked quinoa and sweetcorn kernels in a medium bowl with the
black beans, red pepper, spring onion, olive oil, half of the lime juice, and
half of the chilli; stir to combine. Season with salt and pepper to taste.

4 Put the avocado, garlic, and remaining lime juice in a small bowl; mash
to combine. Season the guacamole with salt and pepper to taste.

5 To assemble the jars, spoon the quinoa mixture into the bottom
of two 3-cup (750ml) jars. Top with the guacamole, sprigs of coriander,
remaining chilli, and a lime wedge for squeezing over. Serve with
tortilla chips, if you like.

TIP

Use canned red kidney beans instead
of black beans, if you like.

Bento box

PREP + COOK TIME **1 HOUR** | SERVES **4**

Bento is the Japanese answer to a packed lunch. Usually based on rice or noodles, it is a balanced meal for one containing carbohydrates, protein, and pickled or cooked vegetables. Our bento box is made up of nori rolls (norikame), with edamame for contrasting crunch.

1 cup (200g) sushi rice

2 tbsp sushi seasoning

2 large plum tomatoes (180g)

2 tbsp soy sauce

5g dried wakame seaweed, ground (see tips)

2 tsp grated fresh root ginger

2 tsp sriracha

1 tsp sesame oil

$^1/_2$ small avocado (100g), cut into cubes

½ small seedless cucumber (50g),
cut into 1cm batons

3 nori sheets (10g)

80g frozen edamame beans with pods, blanched

2 tbsp pink pickled ginger

1 tsp sesame seeds, toasted

1 tbsp vegan mayonnaise (see Everyday Mayo
on page 55 or buy ready-made)

1 Put the rice in a sieve; rinse under cold running water until the water runs clear. Put the rinsed rice in a saucepan with 1½ cups (375ml) water; bring to the boil. Reduce the heat to low; cook, covered, for 10 minutes or until the water is absorbed. Remove the pan from the heat; allow to stand, covered, for 5 minutes. While the rice is still hot, add the sushi seasoning; stir with a fork for 5 minutes or until the rice is sticky and slightly cooled.

2 Score a cross into the bottom of each tomato; place in a heatproof bowl. Pour over boiling water to cover; allow to stand for 1 minute or until the skins start to peel away. Using a slotted spoon, transfer the tomatoes to a bowl of iced water. When cool enough to handle, peel away the skins.

3 Cut the tomatoes in half through the middle; scoop out the seeds and discard. Cut the flesh into 1cm cubes.

4 Whisk together the soy sauce, ground seaweed, ginger, sriracha, and sesame oil in a small bowl until combined. Add the diced tomato; stir to coat. Allow to stand for 30 minutes.

5 Just before making the nori rolls, cut the avocado into cubes and the cucumber into 1cm batons.

6 Place the nori sheet, shiny-side down, on a sushi mat with the long side in front of you. Using damp hands, spread 1 cup of the sticky cooled rice over the nori, leaving a 2cm strip at the top. Place one-third of the tomato mixture, avocado, and cucumber across the centre of the rice. Using the sushi mat, roll up firmly away from you. Dampen the nori strip lightly and seal. Repeat twice more with the remaining ingredients to make 3 nori rolls.

7 Cut each nori roll into 6 pieces. Serve the nori rolls with the edamame, pickled ginger, sesame seeds, and vegan mayonnaise.

TIPS

▪ Use a spice grinder or high-powered mini food processor to grind the seaweed to a coarse powder.
▪ You will need a sushi mat to roll the sushi, found in the cookware aisle of large supermarkets.

Samosa wraps

PREP + COOK TIME **30 MINUTES** | SERVES **2**

The filling for these wraps is inspired by classic potato-and-pea samosas, right down to the accompanying chutney. Mix it up by using orange sweet potato and different varieties of wraps and chutney, if you like.

1 large potato (300g), peeled, cut into 1cm pieces

2 tbsp extra virgin olive oil

$^1/_2$ cup (60g) frozen garden peas

2 tsp curry powder

2 red quinoa or other wholegrain wraps

2 tbsp vegan mayonnaise (see Everyday Mayo on page 55 or buy ready-made)

30g baby spinach leaves

1 seedless cucumber (130g), thinly sliced lengthways

$^1/_2$ small red onion (50g), thinly sliced

$^1/_3$ cup (10g) coriander leaves

2 tbsp mango chutney

$^1/_2$ lime, cut into wedges

1 Boil, steam, or microwave the potato until just tender; drain.

2 Heat the olive oil in a medium frying pan over a high heat; cook the potato, garden peas, and curry powder, stirring, for 3 minutes or until the potatoes are slightly mashed and the peas are hot.

3 Spread the wraps with the mayonnaise; top with the spinach leaves, cucumber, onion, coriander, potato mixture, and chutney. Roll up to enclose the filling. Serve with the lime wedges for squeezing over.

TIPS

- These wraps can be enjoyed warm or cold. For cold wraps, remember to allow the potato filling to cool before assembling.
- Cover the assembled wraps in cling film and refrigerate until ready to eat.
- If you would like to eat these warm but are making them ahead of time, keep the filling and wraps separate; warm the potato filling just before assembling and eating. The potato mixture will keep, refrigerated, for up to 3 days.

Courgette and kale frittatas

PREP + COOK TIME **50 MINUTES** | MAKES **12**

Turmeric and ginger are both powerful anti-inflammatories that aid in the digestion of fats, while leafy greens such as kale provide the vegan eater with an arsenal of nutrients – iron, calcium, and an array of valuable vitamins.

olive oil cooking spray

4 courgettes (480g)

2 tbsp extra virgin olive oil

1 onion (150g), finely chopped

$\frac{1}{2}$ tsp cumin seeds, crushed

$\frac{1}{2}$ tsp fennel seeds, crushed

2 garlic cloves, crushed

2 tbsp grated fresh root ginger

350g purple kale

300g firm tofu, drained of excess liquid

$\frac{1}{2}$ cup (125ml) soy milk

$\frac{1}{3}$ cup (55g) wholemeal plain flour

2 tbsp nutritional yeast flakes

1 tsp ground turmeric

vegan mayonnaise (see Everyday Mayo on page 55 or buy ready-made), to serve

1 Preheat the oven to 160°C (140°C fan/325°F/Gas 3). Grease a 12-hole ($\frac{1}{3}$-cup/80ml) muffin tin; line the bottoms and sides with overlapping squares of baking parchment.

2 Coarsely grate 3 of the courgettes; place in the middle of a piece of muslin or cheesecloth, then twist the ends of the cloth to wring out any excess liquid. (Alternatively, pick up small handfuls of courgette, and squeeze tightly to remove the excess liquid.) Set aside.

3 Heat the olive oil in a frying pan over a medium heat; cook the onion, cumin seeds, and fennel seeds, stirring, for 4 minutes or until the onion softens. Add the garlic and ginger; cook for a further minute or until fragrant.

4 Strip the kale leaves from the stem; discard the stems. You will need 200g kale leaves. Coarsely chop two-thirds of the leaves. Add the chopped kale and grated courgette to the pan with the onion mixture; cook for a further 2 minutes. Allow to cool.

5 Meanwhile, process the tofu, soy milk, flour, nutritional yeast flakes, and turmeric in a food processor until smooth.

6 Combine the tofu mixture and courgette mixture in a large jug. Pour the mixture into the prepared holes of the muffin tin. Using a vegetable peeler, peel the remaining courgette into long, thin ribbons. Roll up the ribbons; top the frittatas with the remaining kale leaves and courgette rolls. Spray with olive oil cooking spray.

7 Bake the frittatas for 20 minutes or until golden and firm. Serve with vegan mayonnaise.

TIPS

- Instead of kale, use the same weight of cavolo nero, which is a straight-leafed form of kale.
- Increase your iron absorption by serving the frittatas with a wedge of lemon.

Tamari noodle jars

PREP + COOK TIME **20 MINUTES** | SERVES **2**

Assembling this layered noodle salad in jars makes this a convenient – and tasty – option for lunch at work or when you're out and about. The tamari sesame dressing soaks into the tofu without making the vegetables soggy, and is easily tossed through when it comes time to eat.

100g dried rice stick noodles

250g firm tofu, cubed

1 cup (80g) finely shredded red cabbage

2 small carrots (140g), cut into julienne or grated

2 tbsp kimchi (see tip)

1 cup (80g) beansprouts

1/2 cup (15g) coriander leaves

1/2 cup (10g) mint leaves

tamari sesame dressing

6cm piece of fresh root ginger

2 tbsp tamari

1 tbsp sesame oil

1 tbsp extra virgin olive oil

1 tbsp rice wine vinegar

1 Cook the noodles in a medium saucepan of boiling water for 6 minutes or until tender. Drain; rinse under running cold water. Set aside.

2 Make the tamari sesame dressing. Peel and finely grate the ginger. Squeeze the grated ginger in your hand over a small bowl to extract the juice; you should have about 1 teaspoon ginger juice. Discard the ginger pulp. Add the remaining ingredients to the bowl; mix to combine.

3 Place the tofu cubes into two 3 1/2-cup (875ml) jars with a lid; pour the dressing over the tofu. Layer with the cabbage, carrot, noodles, kimchi, and beansprouts, then top with the coriander and mint. Cover the jars with their lids. Refrigerate until ready to eat.

4 To serve, pour the contents into a bowl, and toss to combine.

TIPS

• A julienne peeler looks like a wide-bladed vegetable peeler with a serrated rather than straight blade. They are available from kitchenware shops and Asian grocers. Alternatively, cut the carrot into julienne using a mandolin or sharp knife.
• If you don't have kimchi, toss the cabbage in 1 teaspoon rice wine vinegar before layering.

Real 'instant' noodles

Once you have these home-made 'instant' noodles in your repertoire, you may never reach for shop-bought pot noodles again. Chockful of flavour, freshness, and all-round goodness, they leave their pre-packaged compatriots in the shade.

Tofu tom yum

PREP + COOK TIME **5 MINUTES** | SERVES **1**

Place 1 teaspoon vegetarian tom yum paste in a 2-cup (500ml) heatproof jar with a fitted lid. Add 20g dried rice vermicelli noodles, 3 halved cherry tomatoes, 60g diced tofu, 2 torn oyster mushrooms, 1 tablespoon fresh root ginger cut into matchsticks, 1 torn fresh makrut lime leaf, 1 tablespoon beansprouts, and a small handful of coriander leaves. To serve, pour in 1½ cups (375ml) boiling water; stir to combine. Cover with the lid; allow to stand for 3 minutes. Serve with a lime wedge for squeezing over.

Miso ramen noodles

PREP + COOK TIME **5 MINUTES** | SERVES **1**

Stir together 2 teaspoons white miso paste (shiro miso), 1 teaspoon sesame oil, and 1 teaspoon grated fresh root ginger in a 2-cup (500ml) heatproof jar with a fitted lid. Top with 50g cubed silken tofu, ¼ small (17g) carrot cut into julienne, 90g ramen noodles, ¼ cup shelled thawed edamame beans, and 25g enoki mushrooms. To serve, pour in 1½ cups (375ml) boiling water; stir to combine. Cover with the lid; allow to stand for 3 minutes. Serve topped with 1 spring onion sliced on the diagonal.

Green curry noodles

PREP + COOK TIME **5 MINUTES** | SERVES **1**

Stir together 1½ tablespoons bottled vegan green curry paste and ¼ cup (60ml) coconut cream in a 2-cup (500ml) heatproof jar with a fitted lid. Top with 10g brown (or white) rice vermicelli noodles, 20g small broccoli florets, 2 tablespoons frozen garden peas, ¼ cup (10g) baby spinach leaves, and 1 thinly sliced spring onion. To serve, pour in 1½ cups (375ml) boiling water; stir to combine. Cover with the lid; allow to stand for 3 minutes.

Thai curry laksa

PREP + COOK TIME **5 MINUTES** | SERVES **1**

Stir together 1½ tablespoons bottled vegan red curry paste and ¼ cup (60ml) coconut cream in a 2-cup (500ml) heatproof jar with a fitted lid. Top with ½ cup (25g) coarsely shredded Asian greens (such as pak choi, choy sum, or tatsoi), 20g mangetout, 20g fresh thin rice noodles, and 35g fried tofu puffs. To serve, pour in 1½ cups (375ml) boiling water; stir to combine. Cover with the lid; allow to stand for 3 minutes. Serve topped with 1 tablespoon each of fried shallots and Thai basil leaves.

Mushroom and spinach gözleme

PREP + COOK TIME **15 MINUTES** | MAKES **4**

Traditionally, this filled Turkish flatbread is made from hand-rolled dough, but this super-quick version uses ready-made bread wraps instead. Don't forget the squeeze of lemon juice – it makes a big difference to the eating and ensures your gozleme will be at its best!

^{1}/₃ cup (80ml) extra virgin olive oil

1 small onion (80g), finely chopped

2 garlic cloves, crushed

2 tsp ground cumin

2 tsp ground sumac

^{1}/₂ tsp chilli flakes

350g flat mushrooms, thickly sliced

100g Cheddar-style vegan cheese, grated

60g spinach leaves

2 tbsp pine nuts, toasted

4 Mountain Bread or other very thin wraps

olive oil cooking spray

salt and freshly ground black pepper

dill leaves and lemon wedges, to serve

1 Heat 1 tablespoon of the olive oil in a large frying pan over a high heat; cook the onion and garlic, stirring, for 5 minutes or until softened. Stir in the cumin, sumac, and chilli flakes; cook for 1 minute. Transfer the mixture to a bowl.

2 Heat 1½ tablespoons of the olive oil in the same frying pan. Add half of the mushrooms; cook, turning occasionally, for 5 minutes or until golden. Add the cooked mushrooms to the onion mixture. Repeat with the remaining olive oil and mushrooms. Allow the combined mixture to cool for 10 minutes. Stir in the vegan Cheddar, spinach, and pine nuts; season with salt and pepper to taste.

3 Heat a large frying pan over a high heat. Place 2 wraps on a clean work surface. Spread a quarter of the filling mixture down the centre third of each wrap. Fold both sides over to enclose. Spray with olive oil cooking spray. Cook in the pan for 2 minutes on each side or until the cheese melts and the bread is crisp. Using a large spatula, remove from the pan. Cover to keep warm. Repeat with the remaining wraps and filling, spraying with olive oil as needed.

4 Cut each gözleme diagonally, and serve with dill leaves and lemon wedges for squeezing over.

TIP

If you have one, use a sandwich press to cook these super-easy gözleme (as pictured here). Follow steps 1 and 2 as in the method, then sandwich the filling between the Mountain Bread wraps to make 2 large gözleme. Cook in the preheated sandwich press until golden and crisp. Cut into wedges to serve.

Cavolo nero and lentil salad with tempeh chips

PREP + COOK TIME **25 MINUTES** | SERVES **4**

Green lentils are related to the famous French lentils du Puy; these tiny green-blue lentils have a nutty, earthy flavour and a hardy nature that allows them to be rapidly cooked without disintegrating. Green lentils similarly hold their shape well.

1³/₄ cups (350g) dried green lentils

10 cavolo nero leaves (100g), trimmed, shredded

400g mixed baby tomatoes, halved

1 small red onion (80g), quartered, thinly sliced

¹/₄ cup (7g) loosely packed small basil leaves

¹/₄ cup (5g) loosely packed mint leaves

¹/₄ cup (5g) loosely packed flat-leaf parsley leaves

¹/₂ cup (125ml) olive oil

¹/₄ cup (60ml) red wine vinegar

2 tsp Dijon mustard

salt and freshly ground black pepper

tempeh chips

¹/₄ cup (60ml) olive oil

100g tempeh, cut into 3mm slices

1 Cook the lentils in a large saucepan of boiling water, uncovered, for 12 minutes or until just tender; drain. Rinse under cold water; drain well.

2 Meanwhile, make the tempeh chips. Heat the olive oil in a large frying pan over a medium-high heat; cook the tempeh for 1 minute on each side or until golden. Drain on kitchen paper.

3 Arrange the lentils, cavolo nero, tomatoes, onion, and herbs on 4 serving plates or trays.

4 To make the dressing, put the olive oil, red wine vinegar, and Dijon mustard in a screw-top jar with a tight-fitting lid; shake well. Season with salt and pepper to taste.

5 Serve the salad with the tempeh chips and the dressing in small bowls to the side.

TIPS

▪ You can use a mixture of green lentils and Puy lentils, if you like.

▪ Cavolo nero is also known as Tuscan kale. You can use other leafy greens such as kale, Swiss chard, or even spinach instead.

▪ Tempeh, made from fermented soya beans, can be found in the refrigerator section of larger supermarkets and health food shops.

Sweet potato and pea samosas

PREP + COOK TIME **50 MINUTES** | MAKES **8**

Make your own delectable samosa-style pastries filled with spiced sweet potato. You can also make these fragrant, crispy triangles of moreishness with regular potatoes, or use a mixture of potato and sweet potato, if you like.

500g orange sweet potatoes, peeled, cut into 1cm cubes

2 tbsp coconut oil, melted

1/2 onion (75g), finely chopped

2 tsp grated fresh root ginger

2 tsp curry powder

1 cup (120g) frozen garden peas

1/3 cup (50g) sunflower seeds

12 sheets of filo pastry (180g)

1/2 tsp cumin seeds

1/2 tsp sea salt flakes

salt and freshly ground black pepper

lemon wedges, to serve

mint apple raita

1/2 cup (10g) mint leaves

1/4 tsp sea salt flakes

1 cup (280g) coconut yogurt

1 small green apple (130g), cut into julienne

1 Preheat the oven to 200°C (180°C fan/400°F/Gas 6). Line a baking tray with baking parchment.

2 Put the sweet potato in a medium saucepan with enough water to cover; bring to the boil over a high heat. Boil for 5 minutes or until just tender. Drain well.

3 Heat half of the coconut oil in a frying pan over a medium heat; cook the onion, ginger, and curry powder, stirring, for 3 minutes or until fragrant and softened. Add the sweet potatoes and peas; cook, stirring, for 1 minute or until the liquid evaporates. Stir in the sunflower seeds; season with salt and pepper to taste. Allow to cool.

4 Brush 1 sheet of the filo pastry with a little of the remaining coconut oil. Fold in half lengthways, then brush with a little more coconut oil. Place 1/3 cup of the sweet potato mixture at the bottom of one narrow edge of the folded pastry sheet. Fold one corner of the pastry diagonally over the filling to form a triangle. Continue folding to the end of the pastry sheet, retaining the triangular shape. Place on the prepared baking tray; brush with a little more coconut oil. Repeat with the remaining filo, coconut oil, and filling mixture to make a total of 8 samosas. Sprinkle with the cumin seeds and sea salt flakes.

5 Bake the samosas for 15 minutes or until golden and crisp.

6 Make the mint apple raita. Using a mortar and pestle, pound the mint leaves and sea salt to a smooth paste. Stir through the coconut yogurt and apple. If the yogurt is too thick, thin with a little water. Season with pepper to taste.

7 Serve the samosas warm, accompanied by the raita and with lemon wedges for squeezing over.

TIPS

• Use olive oil instead of coconut oil, if you like.

• You can also cook the samosas in a flat sandwich press for 2 minutes or until crisp and lightly golden.

Beetroot and za'atar dip with pitta chips

PREP + COOK TIME **1 HOUR** | SERVES **4 (MAKES 2½ CUPS)**

With its characteristic jewel-like hue, beetroot can't help but be a vivid inclusion in any recipe. Za'atar, a Middle Eastern spice blend, balances the sweetness of beetroot here with its own characteristic balance of herby earthiness and citrussy tartness provided by sumac.

3 large red beetroots (600g), trimmed

¼ cup (60ml) extra virgin olive oil, plus extra 2 tsp

2 large wholemeal pitta breads

1 tbsp pumpkin seeds

½ lemon (70g)

⅔ cup (100g) roasted unsalted cashews

¼ cup (70g) dairy-free yogurt

1½ tsp za'atar

sea salt and freshly ground black pepper

1 Preheat the oven to 180°C (160°C fan/350°F/Gas 4).

2 Scrub the beetroots well. Cut into 1cm cubes. Combine the beetroot and 1 tablespoon of the olive oil on a large baking tray; season with salt and pepper to taste. Roast for 40 minutes; allow to cool.

3 Meanwhile, cut the pitta breads into wedges. Arrange the bread on 2 large baking trays. Brush with the remaining olive oil, and season with sea salt to taste. Bake for 10 minutes or until golden and crisp, turning over halfway through the cooking time. Spread the pumpkin seeds over a medium baking tray; toast for 5 minutes.

4 Remove the zest from the lemon using a zester. (If you don't have a zester, thinly peel the zest from the lemon, avoiding the white pith. Cut the zest into long, thin strips.) Squeeze the juice from the lemon; you will need 1 tablespoon lemon juice.

5 Reserve ¼ cup of the beetroot. Process the remaining beetroot, using the pulse button, until finely chopped. Add the cashews; process until fine. Add the 1 tablespoon lemon juice, yogurt, and 1 teaspoon of the za'atar; pulse until combined. Season with salt and pepper to taste.

6 Transfer the beetroot mixture to a bowl, then drizzle with the extra 2 teaspoons olive oil. Sprinkle with the remaining ½ teaspoon za'atar; top with the reserved beetroot, toasted pumpkin seeds, and lemon zest. Serve the dip with the pitta chips.

TIPS

- Make bread chips from thinly cut bagels instead of pitta bread, if you like.
- Top the dip with pine nuts, chopped almonds, or sunflower seeds instead of pumpkin seeds.
- Serve with crudités such as carrot or radish cut into matchsticks.

Spiced white bean and Greek salad pitta

PREP + COOK TIME **20 MINUTES** | SERVES **4**

Use the recipe below to make your own tofu feta or buy a good-quality feta-style vegan cheese instead. Either way, this is a fantastic option for a portable lunch for work (see tips). Cannellini beans are an excellent source of fibre and protein, so it makes it a filling one too.

1/4 cup (60ml) extra virgin olive oil

1 small red onion (100g), finely chopped

1 garlic clove, crushed

1/4 tsp dried oregano leaves

2 tsp ground cumin

400g can cannellini beans, drained, rinsed (see tips)

1 tbsp freshly squeezed lemon juice

1 tbsp chopped fresh flat-leaf parsley

4 wholemeal pitta breads (420g)

1/3 cup (100g) vegan mayonnaise (see Everyday Mayo on page 55 or buy ready-made)

1/4 cup (40g) pitted kalamata olives, halved

2 baby cucumbers (120g), quartered lengthways

8 golden cherry tomatoes, halved

1 cup (250g) tofu feta (see right or buy ready-made)

salt and freshly ground black pepper

1 lemon, cut into wedges, to serve

1 Heat the olive oil in a large frying pan over a medium heat; cook the onion, stirring, for 3 minutes or until softened. Increase the heat to high. Add the garlic, oregano, cumin, and cannellini beans; cook, stirring, for 2 minutes or until lightly browned. Add the lemon juice and parsley; season with salt and pepper to taste.

2 Meanwhile, warm the pitta breads following the packet directions.

3 Spread the pitta breads with the vegan mayonnaise. Combine the olives, cucumbers, tomatoes, and tofu feta in a medium bowl. Spoon into the pockets with the warm bean mixture.

4 Serve the pitta breads with lemon wedges for squeezing over.

tofu feta You will need to start this recipe a day ahead, to allow time for overnight refrigeration. Whisk together 1/2 cup (125ml) soy milk, 1/3 cup (80ml) rice wine vinegar, 1 tablespoon lemon juice, 1 teaspoon dried oregano, 1 crushed garlic clove, and 2 teaspoons table salt in a large, shallow glass or ceramic dish. Add 375g extra firm tofu, cubed; turn to coat. Cover with cling film; refrigerate overnight. Drain the 'feta' and use straight away, or pat dry and place in a container with 1 teaspoon black peppercorns, 1 tablespoon chopped rosemary, 2 tablespoons torn pitted kalamata olives, and about 2 cups (500ml) olive oil or enough oil to cover; seal. The marinated tofu feta keeps in the fridge for up to 2 weeks (makes about 375g). Alternatively, use one of the variations below.

chilli tofu feta Make the tofu feta as above. Pat dry and put in the container. Omit the black peppercorns, rosemary, and olives. Combine the olive oil with 1 thinly sliced fresh long red chilli, 1 thinly sliced shallot, and 2 sprigs of thyme.

lemon tofu feta Make the tofu feta as above. Pat dry and put in the container. Omit the rosemary and olives. Combine the olive oil and black peppercorns with 3 bay leaves and 3 wide strips of lemon zest.

TIPS

• Save the drained liquid from the canned cannellini beans, called aquafaba, to use in the Everyday Mayo (page 55) or meringues (page 158). You can store it in the fridge for 2 days or freeze for up to 3 months.

• To transport, pack the pitta pockets, mayonnaise, and salad separately; assemble just before serving.

Satay tofu and roast butternut squash wraps

PREP + COOK TIME **40 MINUTES** | SERVES **4-6**

When you are looking for something filling, nutritious, and flavour-filled for lunch, these wraps fit the bill – particularly if you are taking them to work or going on a picnic. To transport, wrap the finished rolls first in baking parchment, then firmly in cling film.

¹/₄ cup (60ml) coconut milk

1 tbsp crunchy natural peanut butter

1 tsp tamari

400g satay tofu, cut into 3cm thick rectangles

400g butternut squash, peeled, cut into 1.5cm thick slices

1 tbsp extra virgin olive oil

4 spinach and herb wraps (see tips)

1 Little Gem or Cos lettuce, trimmed, whole or shredded

1 cup (80g) finely shredded red cabbage

100g mangetout, trimmed, cut into matchsticks

1 red pepper (150g), thinly sliced

1 yellow pepper (150g), thinly sliced

1 red beetroot (150g), peeled, cut into matchsticks

1 avocado (250g)

sprigs of coriander and mint leaves (optional)

salt and freshly ground black pepper

1 Preheat the oven to 200°C (180°C fan/400°F/Gas 6). Line 2 baking trays with baking parchment.

2 Combine the coconut milk, peanut butter, and tamari in a medium bowl. Dip the tofu pieces in the mixture to coat; place on one of the lined trays.

3 Toss the butternut squash in the olive oil; arrange on the remaining tray. Season with salt and pepper to taste. Roast the tofu and squash for 20 minutes, turning halfway through the cooking time, or until golden.

4 Place the wraps on a clean work surface. Divide the lettuce, cabbage, mangetout, peppers, beetroot, tofu, and roast butternut squash among the wraps. Thinly slice the avocado and divide evenly among the wraps. Top with a few sprigs of coriander and mint leaves, if you like. Roll up tightly; cut in half.

TIPS

- The wraps used here are spinach and herb (it's why they're green!), but you can use other wraps such as sweet potato wraps or even multigrain instead.
- Make these into rice paper rolls by substituting rice paper wrappers for the bread wraps. Cut the squash and tofu into smaller pieces, and use at least 8 rounds of rice paper.
- The tofu and butternut squash can be eaten warm if using immediately; if you are making these wraps to go, allow to cool before placing inside the wraps.

Miso peanut bowl with shredded vegetables

PREP + COOK TIME **20 MINUTES** | SERVES **4**

Shiro miso, also known as white miso, is golden in colour. Lighter and mellower than other types, it has a more subtle umami flavour and a nutty sweetness, making it ideal for the dressing. For a more substantial meal, add sliced teriyaki-flavoured or plain tofu, if you like.

1 baby fennel bulb (130g)

1 cup (80g) finely shredded red cabbage

1 cup (80g) finely shredded green cabbage

1 beetroot (150g), peeled, cut into matchsticks

400g baby carrots, trimmed, peeled into ribbons

1/3 cup (45g) finely chopped roasted
unsalted peanuts

1/2 cup (10g) loosely packed mint leaves

1 lime (90g), cut into wedges

miso peanut dressing

1/2 cup (140g) crunchy natural peanut butter

1/4 cup (70g) white miso paste (shiro miso)

2 tbsp coconut sugar

1/2 tsp finely grated lime zest

1 fresh small red chilli, finely chopped

1/3 cup (80ml) lime juice

1 Make the miso peanut dressing. Blend or process the ingredients with 1/2 cup (125ml) water until combined.

2 Thinly slice the fennel bulb and stems (see tips).

3 Divide the fennel, red and green cabbage, beetroot, and carrots among 4 serving bowls; top with the peanuts and mint. Serve with the miso peanut dressing and lime wedges for squeezing over.

TIPS

▪ Use a mandolin or V-slicer for the vegetables for best results. Toss the fennel in lime juice to prevent it from browning if not serving immediately.

▪ Seed the chilli if you prefer less heat.

▪ When travelling, store the dressing and the salad ingredients separately; combine when serving.

Broccoli arancini with rocket and almond pesto

PREP + COOK TIME **50 MINUTES + COOLING** | SERVES **4 (MAKES 16)**

Arancini are a staple of Sicilian cuisine, and this vegan-suitable rendition bears all the classic hallmarks of the traditional dish. The crisp coating encases zesty risotto-style rice, and broccoli brings its own benefits, including a hefty dose of antioxidants such as vitamin C.

3 cups (750ml) vegetable stock

2 tbsp extra virgin olive oil

1 leek (350g), finely chopped

1 garlic clove, crushed

1 cup (200g) arborio rice

1 cup (250ml) dry white wine

150g broccoli, cut into small florets

2 tsp finely grated lemon zest

1¹/₂ cups (110g) packaged gluten-free breadcrumbs (see tips)

grapeseed oil for deep-frying

salt and freshly ground black pepper

rocket and almond pesto

100g rocket, coarsely chopped

¹/₂ cup (80g) roasted almond kernels, coarsely chopped

2 tbsp nutritional yeast flakes

¹/₂ cup (125ml) extra virgin olive oil

TIPS

• Gluten-free breadcrumbs are available from some supermarkets and health food shops. Always check the label first for any dairy products.
• The recipe can be made a day ahead to the end of step 5. Keep the arancini, covered, in the fridge. Store the pesto in a small airtight container, with cling film on the surface, in the fridge.
• Serve with a green leaf or tomato salad and lemon wedges for squeezing over, if you like.

1 Bring the vegetable stock to the boil in a large saucepan. Reduce the heat; simmer, covered.

2 Meanwhile, heat the olive oil in a medium saucepan over a medium heat; cook the leek and garlic, stirring, for 2 minutes or until the leek is soft. Reduce the heat to low. Add the rice; stir to coat the grains in the oil mixture. Add the wine; cook, stirring, for 2 minutes or until the wine is evaporated.

3 Stir in ¹/₂ cup (125ml) of the hot stock; cook, stirring, over a low heat until the liquid is absorbed. Continue adding stock, in ¹/₂-cup (125ml) batches, stirring until the liquid is absorbed after each addition. The total cooking time should be about 20 minutes or until the rice is just tender, with the broccoli being added during the last 10 minutes of cooking. Stir in the lemon zest; season with salt and pepper to taste. Spread the rice mixture over a large baking tray; allow to cool for 15 minutes.

4 With wet hands, roll ¹/₄ cup of the rice mixture into a ball; continue until all the rice is used. Toss the balls in the breadcrumbs to coat; place on a tray. Refrigerate for 30 minutes.

5 Meanwhile, make the rocket and almond pesto. Process the ingredients in a small food processor until almost smooth. Transfer to a small bowl; season with salt and pepper to taste.

6 Fill a large saucepan one-third full with grapeseed oil; heat to 180°C/350°F (or until a cube of bread turns golden in 15 seconds). Deep-fry the balls, in batches, for 2 minutes, turning occasionally, until lightly browned and heated through. Drain on kitchen paper.

7 Serve the arancini with the rocket and almond pesto.

Wasabi edamame hummus pack

PREP + COOK TIME **30 MINUTES** | SERVES **4**

This is a brilliant way to whip up a sharing platter that looks impressive without too much effort. Edamame beans are high in protein, iron, and calcium, while the wasabi paste adds a kick to the hummus. The pairing of edamame and wasabi is a popular one in Japanese cuisine.

1 cup (200g) frozen shelled edamame beans

400g can chickpeas, drained, rinsed

1/4 cup (60ml) lime juice

2 tbsp tahini

1 1/2 tsp wasabi paste

1 small garlic clove, crushed

salt and freshly ground black pepper

extra virgin olive oil, to drizzle

black sesame seeds, to serve (optional)

sesame crisps

12 x 13cm frozen spring roll or rice paper wrappers (see tips)

vegetable oil cooking spray

2 tsp black sesame seeds

1 tsp sea salt flakes

quick pickled vegetables

3/4 cup (180ml) rice wine vinegar

1/2 cup (125ml) pure maple syrup

1/4 cup (60ml) soy sauce

6 radishes (210g), quartered

6 baby cucumbers (180g), quartered lengthways

1 First, make the sesame crisps and quick pickled vegetables. Preheat the oven to 180°C (160°C fan/350°F/Gas 4). Line 2 oven trays with baking parchment. Spray half of the spring roll wrappers with vegetable oil cooking spray. Top with a second wrapper; cut in half to make 12 rectangles. Place the rectangles on the prepared trays; spray with vegetable oil, then sprinkle with the sesame seeds and sea salt. Bake for 10 minutes or until golden. Allow to cool. Break into shards for dipping.

2 To make the quick pickled vegetables, stir together the rice wine vinegar, maple syrup, and soy sauce in a small saucepan until almost simmering. Put the radishes and cucumbers in a medium heatproof bowl; pour the vinegar mixture over the vegetables. Cover; refrigerate for 20 minutes.

3 Put the edamame beans in a colander; place under running hot water until completely thawed. Drain well.

4 Reserve 1 tablespoon of the edamame for serving. Put the remaining edamame in a food processor with the chickpeas, lime juice, tahini, wasabi paste, garlic, and 1/4 cup (60ml) water; process until smooth. Season with salt and pepper to taste.

5 Spoon the dip into a serving bowl; top with the reserved edamame beans. Sprinkle over some black sesame seeds and drizzle with a little olive oil, if you like. Place the dip on a platter with the sesame crisps and pickled vegetables.

TIPS

- You will find spring roll wrappers in the freezer section of the supermarket. Thaw before using.
- The quick pickled vegetables are best made on the day of serving.

King Kong cookies

PREP + COOK TIME **35 MINUTES** | MAKES **20**

Just as their namesake suggests, these are monster-sized cookies to tide you over until your next big meal. Whether it's for a morning snack or a treat in your lunchbox 'just in case', with their satisfying crunch and blend of sweet and salty, they will not disappoint.

2 bananas (400g unpeeled)

2¹/₂ cups (225g) rolled oats

1 cup (75g) shredded coconut

¹/₂ cup (70g) roasted salted peanuts, coarsely chopped

¹/₃ cup (35g) cacao powder, sifted

¹/₂ cup (125ml) pure maple syrup

¹/₄ cup (60ml) extra virgin olive oil

8 soft fresh dates (160g), pitted, finely chopped

¹/₄ cup (35g) cacao nibs (see tips)

1 Preheat the oven to 180°C (160°C fan/350°F/Gas 4). Line 2 baking trays with baking parchment.

2 Mash the bananas in a large bowl until smooth; you will need ³/₄ cup (180g) mashed banana. Add the remaining ingredients, except for the cacao nibs, to the bowl. Using clean hands, mix until well combined.

3 Using damp hands, roll heaped tablespoons of the mixture into balls. Place on the prepared trays. Flatten slightly to 6cm rounds (the cookies will not spread on cooking). Sprinkle with the cacao nibs.

4 Bake the cookies for 20 minutes or until golden brown on the outside. Allow to cool on the trays.

TIPS

• Cacao nibs are fermented crushed dried cacao beans. When they are ground to a liquor, they become the starting point for making chocolate, before sugar and milk are added. They are available from large supermarkets and health food shops.

• Store the cookies in an airtight container at room temperature for up to 3 days, or freeze in airtight bags for up to 1 month.

BIG PLATES

Weeknight suppers, weekend lunches, cosy
nights in, dinner with family or entertaining
friends – from hearty mains to tempting
sides, these meals are made for savouring.

Spicy not-kotsu ramen

PREP + COOK TIME **15 MINUTES + STANDING** | SERVES **4**

This is our playful and flavour-packed vegan take on tonkotsu, traditionally a pork-based dish and one which has its origins in Fukuoka, Japan. Here, shiitake mushrooms impart their characteristic rich umami taste to the broth and up the protein intake alongside the tofu.

¼ cup (60ml) olive oil

2 tsp finely grated fresh root ginger

6 garlic cloves, crushed

4 spring onions, thinly sliced, green tips shredded

2 tbsp spicy black beans in chilli oil

2 tbsp white miso paste (shiro miso) (see tips)

⅓ cup (80ml) mirin

⅓ cup (80ml) soy sauce

2 cups (500ml) soy milk

2 sweetcorn cobs (500g)

4 baby pak choi (240g), halved

270g dried ramen noodles

200g silken tofu, cubed

2 tbsp sesame seeds, toasted, crushed (see tips)

dashi

25g dried shiitake mushrooms

40g dried kombu

1 First, make the dashi. Put the shiitake mushrooms and dried kombu in a large saucepan with 1.5 litres (6 cups) cold tap water; slowly bring to the boil over a low heat. Remove from the heat; allow to stand for 30 minutes for the flavours to infuse. Strain the liquid through a fine sieve into a large jug. Slice the mushrooms, reserving in a small bowl; discard the kombu.

2 Heat the olive oil in a large saucepan over a medium heat; cook the ginger, garlic, and sliced spring onions for 4 minutes or until softened. Add the black beans and miso; cook, stirring, for 1 minute. Add the mirin and soy sauce; bring to the boil.

3 Reduce the heat to medium. Add the reserved dashi and the soy milk; cook for 5 minutes or until just below boiling point. Strain through a fine sieve; discard the solids. Stir in the reserved sliced shiitake mushrooms.

4 Meanwhile, bring a large saucepan of water to the boil. Cook the sweetcorn for 5 minutes or until tender; remove with tongs. Add the pak choi to the water; cook for 2 minutes or until tender, then remove with tongs. Add the noodles to the same water; cook for 5 minutes or until tender. Drain. Cut the kernels from the sweetcorn cobs.

5 Divide the noodles and pak choi evenly among 4 serving bowls. Pour over the hot broth. Top with the sweetcorn kernels, shredded spring onion, and tofu. Serve sprinkled with the sesame seeds.

TIPS

- Always check the ingredients listed on miso pastes, as some brands contain bonito (tuna) extract, which is unsuitable for vegans.
- To toast sesame seeds, stir continuously in a small frying pan over a medium heat until golden. Crush using a mortar and pestle.

Beet Wellington

PREP + COOK TIME **3 HOURS 20 MINUTES** | SERVES **6**

It is important to buy beetroots that are equal in size for this recipe, so that the pastry encases them snugly and your Wellington looks at its most elegant.

6 large beetroots (1.2kg in total), scrubbed (see tips)

$1/4$ cup (60ml) extra virgin olive oil

1 tbsp sherry vinegar

1 tbsp fresh thyme leaves

4 shallots, finely chopped

2 cups (200g) walnuts, toasted, coarsely chopped

2 tbsp flaxseed meal

1 tsp ground nutmeg

$1/3$ cup (80ml) white wine

240g baby spinach leaves

3 sheets of frozen puff pastry

1 tbsp almond milk

1 tsp caster sugar

salt and freshly ground black pepper

TIPS

• Beetroot leaves are edible. If you buy beetroots with the leaves still attached, trim and wash the young leaves. Blanch in a saucepan of boiling water until just wilted; drain. Toss the leaves with a little olive oil; season with salt and freshly ground black pepper. Serve alongside the beet Wellington.

• Serve with mashed potato and a horseradish cream; for horseradish cream, combine 1 teaspoon prepared horseradish with $1/3$ cup (80ml) vegan mayonnaise or dairy-free yogurt.

1 Preheat the oven to 200°C (180°C fan/400°F/Gas 6). Line a small roasting tin and a large baking tray with baking parchment.

2 Put the beetroots in the prepared roasting tin. Drizzle with 1 tablespoon of the olive oil and the sherry vinegar. Scatter over half of the thyme leaves; season generously with salt and pepper. Cover the tin with baking parchment, then foil; seal well. Roast the beetroot for 1 hour 20 minutes or until cooked through. Allow to cool; peel, then trim the ends.

3 Meanwhile, heat the remaining olive oil in a small frying pan over a medium heat; cook the shallots for 10 minutes. Add the walnuts, flaxseed meal, nutmeg, and remaining thyme. Stir in the wine and $1/4$ cup (60ml) water; cook for 2 minutes. Season with salt and pepper to taste. Cool.

4 Blanch the spinach in salted boiling water for 20 seconds; drain, then refresh in iced water. Drain again, squeezing out all the water you can. Pat dry with kitchen paper to help absorb any excess moisture. Set aside.

5 Cut one of the pastry sheets in half, then join each half to a whole pastry sheet; press along the join to seal. Next, join the 2 extended pieces of pastry to each other by overlapping down a long side to form a 36cm x 48cm rectangle of pastry.

6 Spread the cooled walnut mixture in the middle of the pastry, leaving an 8cm border on the long sides and a 3cm border on the short sides. Press to compact the mixture, then top with the reserved spinach, unravelling it slightly so that it sits flat. Place the beetroots upright on top, arranging them in a line next to each other. Trim away any excess pastry if needed, then roll the pastry over the beetroots to enclose the filling. Tuck the ends under, and place on the lined large baking tray.

7 Brush the pastry generously with the combined almond milk and caster sugar. Using a sharp knife, score the top; sprinkle with pepper. Bake for 40 minutes, rotating the tray halfway through the cooking time.

8 Serve the beet Wellington in slices.

Carrot and millet patties with sunflower slaw

PREP + COOK TIME **45 MINUTES** | SERVES **2**

Millet, a small, nutrient-dense seed, is packed with fibre, protein, B vitamins, and minerals –
as are sunflower seeds. Serve with a minty mayonnaise alongside, if you like.

1 cup (250ml) vegetable stock

½ cup (100g) millet

1 shallot, finely chopped

$^1/_3$ cup (50g) sun-dried tomatoes,
finely chopped

1 carrot (120g), finely grated

1 tbsp tomato purée

1 tbsp freshly squeezed lemon juice

salt and freshly ground black pepper

lemon wedges, to serve

sunflower slaw

2 tbsp freshly squeezed lemon juice

$^1/_4$ cup (60ml) extra virgin olive oil

2 tsp Dijon mustard

2 cups (160g) finely shredded green cabbage

1 cup (80g) finely shredded red cabbage

½ cup (10g) mint leaves

$^1/_4$ cup (40g) sunflower seeds

1 Preheat the oven to 200°C (180°C fan/400°F/Gas 6). Line a baking tray
with baking parchment.

2 Bring the vegetable stock to the boil in a small saucepan. Reduce the
heat to low; partially cover with a lid.

3 Stir the millet in a medium saucepan over a medium heat for 3 minutes
or until fragrant and toasted. Add the hot stock to the millet, stir well.
Bring to the boil. Reduce the heat to low; cook the millet, covered, for
15 minutes or until the liquid is absorbed.

4 Transfer the millet to a food processor. Add the shallot, sun-dried
tomatoes, carrot, tomato purée, and lemon juice. Season with salt and
pepper to taste. Pulse until the mixture comes together but still has
some texture.

5 Shape about $^1/_4$ cup each of the millet mixture into four 8cm patties;
place on the lined tray. Bake for 20 minutes or until golden and crisp.

6 To make the sunflower slaw, blend the lemon juice, olive oil, and Dijon
mustard in a blender until smooth. Season with salt and pepper to taste.
Put the green and red cabbage, mint, and 2 tablespoons of the sunflower
seeds in a medium bowl with the dressing; toss well to combine. Sprinkle
with the remaining sunflower seeds.

7 Serve the patties with the sunflower slaw, with lemon wedges for
squeezing over and a fresh mint mayonnaise (see tips), if you like.

TIPS

• You can make the dressing, shred the cabbage, and
shape the patties (or even bake them) a day ahead.
Store each ingredient separately in the fridge.
Reheat the patties before serving.

• Serve with vegan mayonnaise (see Everyday Mayo,
page 55) blended with 2 tablespoons coarsely
chopped mint leaves and 2 teaspoons lemon juice.

Mushroom, spinach, and walnut pasta

PREP + COOK TIME **20 MINUTES** | SERVES **2**

Spelt, used here for the pasta, is an ancient grain with similarities to wheat. Unlike plain flour, which is refined by removing the germ and the bran, the nutritious part of the spelt grain remains when it's milled into wholemeal flour.

¹/₃ cup (80ml) extra virgin olive oil

¹/₂ cup (50g) walnuts

125g dried spelt fusilli pasta (see tips)

150g Asian mixed mushrooms, sliced (see tips)

2 garlic cloves, finely chopped

1 long red chilli, seeded, finely chopped

2 tsp apple cider vinegar

280g baby spinach leaves, washed

salt and freshly ground black pepper

1 Heat 1 tablespoon of the olive oil in a small frying pan over a medium heat; cook the walnuts, stirring continuously, for 5 minutes or until golden and toasted. Remove from the pan; allow to cool. Coarsely chop the nuts. Set aside.

2 Cook the pasta in a large saucepan of boiling salted water for 12 minutes or until almost tender. Drain. Return the pasta to the pan off the heat; cover and keep warm until needed.

3 Meanwhile, heat the remaining olive oil in a medium saucepan over a medium-high heat; cook the mushrooms for 2 minutes or until tender and golden. Add the garlic and chilli; cook stirring, for 1 minute or until fragrant. Add the cider vinegar; cook for 1 minute. Add the spinach and toasted walnuts; cook for 1 minute or until the spinach is lightly wilted. Season with salt and pepper to taste.

4 Add the mushroom-spinach mixture to the pasta; toss well to coat the pasta. Serve immediately.

TIPS

- You can use any shaped spelt pasta for this recipe.
- Packs of Asian mixed mushrooms often include a combination of king brown, enoki, shiitake, oyster, and shimeji mushrooms. You can make up your own flavourful mixture, if you like.

Sweet and spicy tofu noodles

PREP + COOK TIME **30 MINUTES** | SERVES **2**

Fresh ginger and chilli add a kick to this simple stir-fry, while crispy fried shallots finish everything off with a crunch. You can also serve this dish topped with sliced chilli, chopped peanuts, and lime wedges for squeezing over, if you like.

200g dried rice stick noodles

250g firm tofu

1 tbsp groundnut oil

1 garlic clove, crushed

1 tbsp finely chopped fresh root ginger

250g packet fresh stir-fry vegetables

1/4 cup (60ml) sweet chilli sauce

2 tbsp sriracha

2 tsp tamari

50g beansprouts, plus extra, to serve

2 tbsp fried shallots

1/3 cup (10g) loosely packed coriander leaves

1 Put the noodles in a large heatproof bowl; pour in enough boiling water to cover. Allow to stand for 5 minutes or until the noodles soften. Drain.

2 Meanwhile, pat the tofu dry with kitchen paper, to remove as much moisture as possible. Cut the tofu into 2cm cubes.

3 Heat the groundnut oil in a wok or large frying pan over a medium-high heat. Add the tofu; cook for 1 minute on each side or until golden. Remove with a slotted spoon. Add the garlic, ginger, and stir-fry vegetables to the wok; cook for 1 minute or until the vegetables are just starting to soften.

4 Add the drained noodles, combined sauces, and the 50g beansprouts; stir-fry gently to prevent the noodles breaking up, until just combined and heated through.

5 Divide the mixture between 2 serving bowls. Top with the tofu, extra beansprouts, fried shallots, and coriander.

TIPS

- To make your own stir-fry mix, combine broccoli florets, sugarsnap peas, and red pepper strips.
- Fried shallots are a popular garnish in Southeast Asian cooking, and are readily available from Asian grocers. Make sure to seek out a good-quality brand – or make your own, if you like.

Lunch bowls

These nutritious bowls are a fast answer to what to do for lunch or supper. Recipe quantities can easily be halved or doubled. Experiment with different grains and vegetables, if you like.

Rainbow avocado bowl

PREP TIME **10 MINUTES** | SERVES **2**

In a small bowl, stir 1 tablespoon tahini, 1¹/₂ tablespoons water, 1 tablespoon lemon juice, and 2 teaspoons extra virgin olive oil until well combined. Set aside. Halve 1 large avocado (320g), and place the halves cut-side up on a plate. Fill each half with ¹/₂ small carrot (25g), cut into julienne or grated, ¹/₂ small beetroot (50g), cut into julienne or grated, 2 tablespoons kimchi, and 1 tablespoon pea shoots, if you like. Season with salt and freshly ground black pepper to taste. Drizzle with the lemon tahini dressing.

Mixed-grain bowl

PREP + COOK TIME **20 MINUTES** | SERVES **2**

Process 2 tablespoons tahini, ¹/₄ cup (8g) basil, 3 teaspoons white wine vinegar, and ¹/₂ cup (125ml) water until smooth. Season with salt and freshly ground black pepper. Set aside. Heat 2 tablespoons extra virgin olive oil in a large frying pan over a medium-high heat. Add 1 crushed garlic clove; cook for 30 seconds. Add 250g microwave brown rice and quinoa; cook, stirring, for 5 minutes until starting to crisp. Transfer to a bowl to keep warm. Add 1 tablespoon extra virgin olive oil to the same pan; cook 300g halved Brussels sprouts, turning occasionally, for 5 minutes until tender and charred. Transfer to a plate; keep warm. Add another 1 tablespoon extra virgin olive oil to the pan. Cook 150g cavolo nero, turning, for 2 minutes or until just starting to wilt. Transfer to a plate; keep warm. Divide the rice mixture between 2 bowls; top with the Brussels sprouts, cavolo nero, 1 sliced avocado (250g), ¹/₄ cup (50g) pumpkin seeds, the tahini dressing, and 1 tablespoon basil leaves.

Miso cashew bowl

PREP + COOK TIME **20 MINUTES + 4 HOURS' STANDING** | SERVES **4**

Put 1 cup (150g) raw cashews in a small bowl; cover with water. Allow to stand, covered, for 4 hours; drain. Blend with 2 tablespoons white miso paste, 2 tablespoons coconut sugar, ¹/₂ teaspoon finely grated lime zest, 1 small chopped red chilli, ¹/₃ cup (80ml) lime juice, and ¹/₂ cup (125ml) water in a high-powered blender until smooth. Thinly slice 1 baby fennel bulb (130g); toss in a little lime juice. Divide the fennel, 2 cups (160g) finely shredded red cabbage, 400g baby carrots, peeled into ribbons, and 1 beetroot (150g), cut into matchsticks, among 4 bowls. Top with ¹/₃ cup (45g) finely chopped raw cashews and ¹/₂ cup (10g) mint leaves. Serve with the miso cashew dressing, sliced red chilli, and lime wedges.

Spicy soba noodle bowl

PREP + COOK TIME **20 MINUTES** | SERVES **2**

Cut 1 spring onion into 6cm lengths, then into long strips; put in a bowl of iced water to curl. Combine ¹/₂ teaspoon dried chilli flakes, 2 crushed small garlic cloves, 2 tablespoons tamari, 2 tablespoons Chinese black vinegar, 1 tablespoon sesame oil, and 2 thinly sliced spring onions in a small bowl. Bring a saucepan of salted water to the boil over a high heat. Cook 500g halved choi sum (500g) for 1 minute until just tender. Remove with tongs; place on a plate. Drizzle with 1 tablespoon sesame oil. Add 180g dried green tea soba noodles to the boiling water; cook for 3 minutes. Add 250g thawed frozen shelled edamame; cook for 1 minute to heat through. Drain; return to the pan. Gently toss through the chilli-garlic sauce. Serve topped with the spring onion curls and toasted sesame seeds.

Coconut and split pea curry

PREP + COOK TIME **1 HOUR 20 MINUTES** | SERVES **4**

Split peas are a nutrient-dense legume containing fibre, iron, protein, minerals, and vitamins A and B to support a good immune system and eyesight, assist in red blood cell production, and help to convert energy from the foods we eat. Serve the curry with brown rice, if you like.

1 cup (200g) yellow split peas

600g kabocha squash such as Kent, peeled, seeded, cut into 3cm cubes

¼ cup (60ml) olive oil, plus extra, to grease

1 large onion (200g), diced

1 tsp finely grated fresh root ginger

4 garlic cloves, crushed

1 tbsp garam masala

1 litre (4 cups) vegetable stock

270ml canned coconut cream

250g green beans, trimmed

1 tbsp freshly squeezed lime juice

salt and freshly ground black pepper

to serve

coriander leaves

mint leaves

nigella seeds

lime wedges

1 Put the split peas in a large heatproof bowl with enough boiling water to cover. Allow to stand until needed.

2 Preheat the oven to 220°C (200°C fan/425°F/Gas 7). Oil and line a large baking tray.

3 Arrange the kabocha squash in a single layer on the prepared baking tray; drizzle with a little of the olive oil. Season with salt and pepper to taste. Roast for 25 minutes or until golden.

4 Meanwhile, heat the remaining olive oil in a large saucepan over a medium heat. Cook the onion for 4 minutes or until softened. Add the ginger and garlic; cook for 1 minute. Stir in the garam masala; cook for a further minute or until fragrant.

5 Add the drained split peas and vegetable stock to the saucepan. Increase the heat to high; cook, stirring frequently, for 30 minutes or until the split peas are soft and the curry is thick.

6 Reduce the heat to medium. Add the coconut cream, green beans, and roasted squash; stir to combine. Simmer for 2 minutes or until the beans are just tender. Stir through the lime juice; season with salt and pepper to taste.

7 Serve the curry topped with coriander, mint, and nigella seeds, with lime wedges for squeezing over. Or keep it simple and serve without the toppings, if you like.

Mushroom 'steak' sandwich

PREP + COOK TIME **20 MINUTES** | SERVES **2**

Mushrooms' umami flavour and dense, meaty texture make them ideal for this sandwich.
This lazy recipe is easy on the hip pocket, too, with only a few fresh ingredients needed.

$^1/_4$ cup (60ml) extra virgin olive oil

1 large onion (200g), thinly sliced

1 large green pepper (350g), thinly sliced

375g portobello mushrooms, sliced

2 garlic cloves, crushed

2 tbsp smoky barbecue sauce

$^1/_3$ cup (80ml) vegan beef-like stock (see tips)

2 slices of Cheddar-style vegan cheese (36g), halved

2 long seeded bread rolls (100g), split in half

2 tbsp American-style mustard

salt and freshly ground black pepper

fresh or pickled sliced jalapeño chillies,
to serve (optional)

1 Heat the olive oil in a large non-stick frying pan over a high heat; cook the onion and green pepper for 4 minutes or until softened. Add the mushrooms; cook, stirring, for 5 minutes or until golden. Add the garlic; stir for 1 minute. Add the barbecue sauce and vegan stock; cook for 2 minutes or until thickened. Season with salt and pepper to taste.

2 Place the vegan Cheddar in the bread rolls; spoon the hot mushroom mixture on top. Drizzle with the mustard; top with sliced jalapeño chillies, if you like.

TIPS

▪ Mushrooms have a low calorific density and contain an important mix of minerals and vitamins. They are also one of the leading plant-based sources of selenium, an antioxidant that assists in warding off chronic diseases.

▪ There is an assortment of vegan stocks available that mimic chicken and beef flavours; these are labelled beef- or chicken-'like' and contain no animal products.

Bliss and chips with mushy peas

PREP + COOK TIME **1 HOUR + STANDING + REFRIGERATION** | SERVES **4**

For all the fun of fish and chips without the fish, our battered aubergine is a delicious stand-in. With their long, finger-like shape, Japanese aubergines work well in grilled and fried dishes, and are usually less bitter and have fewer seeds than their European counterparts.

4 Japanese aubergines (460g)

1 tbsp fine sea salt

4 nori sheets (10g), halved

1¼ cups (190g) self-raising flour

1½ cups (375ml) pale ale

750g potatoes, scrubbed, unpeeled

2 tbsp extra virgin olive oil

vegetable oil for shallow-frying

salt and freshly ground black pepper

1 large lemon (200g), cut into cheeks, to serve

tartare sauce

4 cornichons

1 spring onion

1 cup (300g) vegan mayonnaise
(use Everyday Mayo on page 55 or buy ready-made)

2 tbsp baby capers

mushy peas

2 cups (240g) frozen garden peas

50g vegan margarine spread

4 sprigs of mint

1 tbsp freshly squeezed lemon juice

1   Preheat the oven to 200°C (180°C fan/400°F/Gas 4). Line 2 baking trays with baking parchment.

2   Halve the aubergines lengthways; place in a colander. Sprinkle with salt; allow to stand for 30 minutes. Rinse the aubergines under cold water. Gently squeeze out any excess water.

3   Wrap each aubergine half in a piece of nori (the moisture will help the nori stick to the aubergine). Refrigerate for 15 minutes.

4   Make the tartare sauce. Finely chop the cornichons and spring onion. Combine with the mayonnaise and capers in a small bowl.

5   Next, make the mushy peas. Cook the garden peas, margarine, and mint in a small saucepan over a medium heat for 6 minutes or until tender. Discard the mint. Using a hand-held blender, pulse the peas, leaving some whole. Season with salt and pepper to taste; stir in the lemon juice.

6   Put 1¼ cups (190g) of the flour in a bowl; season with salt and pepper. Gradually whisk in the beer to make a smooth batter. Allow to stand at room temperature for 30 minutes.

7   Cut the unpeeled potatoes into chunky chips. Place the chips on the prepared baking trays; drizzle with the olive oil, then season with salt and pepper to taste. Bake for 30 minutes or until golden and crisp.

8   Meanwhile, fill a large saucepan or deep-fryer one-third full with vegetable oil; heat to 170°C/340°F (or until a cube of bread turns golden in 8 seconds). Dust the aubergine halves in the remaining ¼ cup (35g) flour. Dip into the batter, allowing any excess to drain off. Fry, in two batches, for 3 minutes each or until golden, turning halfway through the cooking time. Drain on a wire rack lined with kitchen paper.

9   Serve the aubergines with the chips, mushy peas, tartare sauce, and lemon cheeks for squeezing over.

Pulled jackfruit bao buns

PREP + COOK TIME **40 MINUTES** | SERVES **4**

A large tropical fruit with a meaty texture and neutral taste, jackfruit readily absorbs other flavours and can be used in sweet and savoury dishes. It is also a good source of protein, fibre, and antioxidants, as well as vitamins and minerals such as vitamin C and manganese.

565g can young green jackfruit in brine (see tips), drained, rinsed

$\frac{1}{2}$ cup (130g) hoisin sauce

2 tbsp pure maple syrup

2 tbsp tamari

$\frac{1}{4}$ tsp Chinese five-spice powder

1 Lebanese or other small seedless cucumber (130g), thinly sliced

1 long red chilli, thinly sliced

2 tbsp rice wine vinegar

8 frozen mini mantou buns (180g) (see tips)

2 tbsp vegan mayonnaise (use Everyday Mayo on page 55 or buy ready-made)

1 spring onion, thinly sliced

$\frac{1}{3}$ cup (10g) coriander leaves

$\frac{1}{3}$ cup (50g) roasted salted peanuts, finely chopped

salt and freshly ground black pepper

1 Cut the jackfruit into 1cm slices through the core. Combine the hoisin sauce, $\frac{1}{4}$ cup (60ml) water, maple syrup, tamari, and five-spice powder in a medium saucepan over a medium heat. Season with pepper to taste. Add the jackfruit; bring to a simmer. Cook for 20 minutes, stirring and breaking up the jackfruit with the back of a spoon, until the sauce has thickened and the mixture resembles pulled pork.

2 Meanwhile, combine the cucumber, chilli, and rice wine vinegar in a medium glass or stainless-steel bowl; season with salt and pepper to taste. Allow to stand for 5 minutes; drain.

3 Split the frozen buns three-quarters of the way through. Steam the buns, covered, in a bamboo steamer over a saucepan of simmering water for 5 minutes or until puffed up and heated through.

4 Spread the buns with the mayonnaise; fill with the jackfruit mixture, pickled cucumber mixture, spring onion, coriander, and peanuts.

TIPS

- Canned jackfruit can be found at Asian supermarkets and grocers. Ensure that you are buying jackfruit in brine, not syrup.
- Mantou, a type of steamed white bun popular in northern Chinese cuisine, are available frozen from Asian supermarkets. You can serve the pulled jackfruit in wraps or other soft buns, if you like.

Courgette noodles with cashew pesto

PREP + COOK TIME **20 MINUTES + STANDING** | SERVES **2**

There are several methods you can use to make the courgette noodles (see tips). You can also make your own Parmesan-style vegan cheese to go with them using the recipe below.

4 large courgettes (600g in total)

125g mixed heirloom cherry tomatoes, halved

1/4 cup (7g) basil leaves

1 tbsp pine nuts

2 tbsp Parmesan-style vegan cheese
(use the recipe at right or buy ready-made)

salt and freshly ground black pepper

cashew pesto

2/3 cup (100g) raw cashews

1 cup (50g) firmly packed basil leaves

1/4 cup (40g) pine nuts

2 tbsp freshly squeezed lemon juice

1/4 cup (60ml) extra virgin olive oil

2 tsp nutritional yeast flakes

1 garlic clove, crushed

1 To make the cashew pesto, put the cashews in a small bowl with enough cold water to cover. Allow to stand for 2 hours. Drain, rinse under cold water; drain well. Process the drained cashews with the basil, pine nuts, lemon juice, olive oil, nutritional yeast flakes, and garlic until smooth. Season with salt and pepper to taste.

2 Using a spiralizer or julienne peeler, cut the courgettes into 'noodles'; place in a large bowl.

3 Add the pesto and cherry tomatoes to the bowl; toss to combine. Top with the basil leaves, pine nuts, and Parmesan-style vegan cheese. Season with salt and pepper to taste. Serve immediately.

vegan Parmesan Process 3/4 cup (115g) raw cashews, 1/3 cup (25g) nutritional yeast flakes, 3/4 teaspoon sea salt flakes, and 1/4 teaspoon garlic powder into a fine meal, similar in consistency to finely grated Parmesan cheese. Store in an airtight container in the fridge for up to 2 months. Use like regular Parmesan.

TIPS

- Store any leftover pesto in an airtight container in the fridge for up to 1 week. Spread leftover pesto on toast or seeded crackers for a delicious snack.
- A spiralizer is a hand-cranked machine designed to cut vegetables into noodles or ribbons. A julienne peeler, a wide-bladed vegetable peeler with a serrated rather than straight blade, is another option. Both are available from kitchenware shops.
- If you don't have a spiralizer or julienne peeler, peel the courgettes into long ribbons, stack on top of one another, and cut into long, thin strips.

Coconut, tomato, and lentil soup

PREP + COOK TIME **30 MINUTES** | SERVES **4**

Save even more time and money, and make a double batch of this comforting soup to freeze.
Its warmth will definitely not go amiss during cold weather. Tempering the spices in the onion
base brings out their essential oils and their full flavour and aroma.

1 tbsp coconut oil

1 small onion (80g), thinly sliced

2 tsp yellow mustard seeds

2 tsp curry powder

2 tbsp tomato purée

1 cup (200g) red lentils

1 litre (4 cups) vegetable stock

$^1/_2$ cup (125ml) coconut milk,
plus extra, to drizzle

2 tomatoes (300g)

salt and freshly ground black pepper

sprigs of coriander leaves
and lemon wedges, to serve

1 Heat the coconut oil in a medium saucepan over a medium-high heat;
cook the onion, stirring, for 3 minutes or until soft. Add the mustard
seeds; stir for 4 minutes or until they start to pop. Add the curry powder;
cook, stirring, for 1 minute. Add the tomato purée; cook, stirring, for a
further 30 seconds.

2 Add the lentils, vegetable stock, and coconut milk; bring to the boil.
Reduce the heat to low; simmer, covered, for 10 minutes, stirring
occasionally, or until the lentils are tender. Coarsely chop one of the
tomatoes; stir into the soup until just heated through. Season with salt
and pepper to taste.

3 Ladle the soup into 4 serving bowls; drizzle with a little extra coconut
milk, then top each serving with the remaining coarsely chopped tomato
and a few coriander leaves. Serve with lemon wedges for squeezing over.

TIPS

- Turn this soup into a curry by reducing the quantity
of stock by 1 cup (250ml). You could also serve the
soup topped with coarsely chopped smoked
almonds or crushed poppadoms.
- The soup can be frozen at the end of step 2. Freeze
in airtight containers for up to 1 month. Thaw and
gently reheat.

Spaghetti with mushroom 'meatballs'

PREP + COOK TIME **1 HOUR + REFRIGERATION** | SERVES **4**

These 'meatballs' are powered by the incredibly satisfying and hearty taste of mushrooms.
Serve sprinkled with vegan Parmesan, if you like (to make your own, see page 112).

¼ cup (60ml) extra virgin olive oil,
plus extra 4 tbsp

1 large onion (200g), finely chopped

600g chestnut mushrooms, finely chopped

4 garlic cloves, crushed

2 tsp dried oregano

1 cup (100g) fresh breadcrumbs

⅔ cup (60g) rolled oats

400g can chickpeas, drained, rinsed

25g dried shiitake mushrooms, grated (see tip)

⅓ cup (10g) finely chopped flat-leaf parsley

¼ cup (40g) plain flour

400g dried spaghetti

salt and freshly ground black pepper

marinara sauce

2 tbsp extra virgin olive oil

1 large onion (200g), finely chopped

4 garlic cloves, crushed

1 long red chilli, seeded, finely chopped

1 tsp dried oregano

½ cup (125ml) dry white wine

3 x 400g cans crushed tomatoes

TIP

Use a Microplane grater to finely grate the dried shiitake mushrooms; alternatively, grind them to a fine powder using a high-powered spice grinder or blender.

1   Heat the ¼ cup (60ml) olive oil in a large frying pan over a high heat; cook the onion for 4 minutes or until golden. Add the chopped mushrooms and 2 tablespoons of the extra olive oil; cook for 10 minutes or until all liquid has evaporated and the mushrooms are golden.

2   Add the garlic and oregano; cook for a further minute. Remove from the heat; allow to cool for 5 minutes. In a food processor, pulse the mushroom mixture with the breadcrumbs, rolled oats, chickpeas, shiitake mushrooms and ¼ cup (7g) of the parsley until combined. Season with salt and pepper to taste. Pulse until the mixture is pasty.

3   Dust a large tray with half of the flour. Using lightly damp hands, roll heaped tablespoonfuls of the mixture into 24 balls; place the 'meatballs' on the floured tray. Sift the remaining flour over the meatballs. Refrigerate, uncovered, for 2 hours or until firm.

4   Meanwhile, make the marinara sauce. Heat the olive oil in a medium saucepan over a medium heat; cook the onion for 4 minutes or until softened. Add the garlic, chilli, and oregano; cook for a further minute or until fragrant. Increase the heat to high. Add the wine; cook for a minute or until evaporated. Add the tomatoes; bring to the boil. Reduce the heat to medium; simmer for 15 minutes or until slightly thickened. Season with salt and pepper to taste.

5   Heat the remaining 2 tablespoons of extra olive oil for the meatballs in a large, non-stick frying pan over a medium heat. Cook the meatballs, in batches, for 6 minutes, gently shaking the pan occasionally, until evenly browned. Add the marinara sauce to the pan; toss very gently to combine and warm through, taking care not to break up the meatballs.

6   Meanwhile, cook the spaghetti in a large saucepan of boiling water for 12 minutes or until almost tender; drain.

7   Serve the spaghetti topped with the meatball mixture and sprinkled with the remaining parsley.

Tandoori tofu kebabs with mint yogurt sauce

PREP + COOK TIME **35 MINUTES** | MAKES **4**

This summery dish couldn't be easier to make and is ideal for an alfresco lunch or supper on a balmy evening. Remember to check the back label of the coconut yogurt for its entire list of ingredients, as sugar is not always declared on the front.

olive oil cooking spray

500g firm tofu

1 red pepper (200g)

1 red onion (170g)

2 tomatoes (300g)

2 tbsp tandoori paste

1/3 cup (95g) unsweetened dairy-free coconut yogurt (see tips)

1 tbsp small mint leaves

lime wedges, to serve

mint yogurt sauce

1/2 cup (140g) unsweetened dairy-free coconut yogurt (see tips)

2 tbsp finely chopped mint leaves

1/4 cup (60ml) freshly squeezed lime juice

1 Preheat an oiled ridged cast-iron grill pan (or barbecue flat plate) to medium-high. Soak 4 bamboo skewers in cold water to prevent them from scorching.

2 Using kitchen paper, pat the tofu dry well, then cut into 2cm x 4cm pieces. Remove the seeds from the pepper. Cut the pepper and red onion each into eight 4cm pieces. Cut the tomatoes into quarters.

3 Combine the paste and coconut yogurt in a medium bowl. Add the tofu; stir gently until evenly coated.

4 Thread the pepper, onion, tomatoes, and tofu onto the skewers, alternating the ingredients. Cook the kebabs for 5 minutes on each side or until the vegetables are tender and the tofu is golden.

5 To make the mint yogurt sauce, process the coconut yogurt, mint, and lime juice in a small food processor until smooth. (Alternatively, mix together the ingredients in a small bowl.)

6 Serve the tofu kebabs accompanied by the mint yogurt sauce, with the mint leaves sprinkled over the top and lime wedges for squeezing over.

TIPS

▪ These kebabs are a little on the spicy side; you may want to adjust the quantity of tandoori paste if you prefer a little less spice.

▪ The Home-made Coconut Yogurt on page 21 can be used for the mint yogurt sauce, if you like, but is not suitable for coating the tofu because of the cooking.

▪ If you like, you can cook the kebabs in a preheated 220°C (200°C fan/425°F/Gas 7) oven for 30 minutes or until browned, turning the kebabs over halfway through the cooking time.

Vegan mac 'n' cheese

PREP + COOK TIME **50 MINUTES** | SERVES **4**

Macaroni and cheese is the ultimate comfort food, and now those going dairy-free can enjoy it, too, with this vegan macaroni and cheese. The 'cheese' sauce part of the recipe can also be used to make a simple baked dish by layering with chargrilled aubergine.

500g dried macaroni

30g vegan margarine

¼ cup (40g) plain flour

1 tsp smoked paprika

¼ tsp cayenne pepper

¼ tsp garlic powder

3 cups (750ml) macadamia milk (see tips)

225g grated mozzarella-style vegan cheese (use the vegan mozzarella recipe on page 26 or buy ready-made)

²⁄₃ cup (55g) grated Parmesan-style vegan cheese (use the vegan Parmesan recipe on page 112 or buy ready-made)

1 tbsp nutritional yeast flakes

salt and freshly ground black pepper

finely chopped chives or flat-leaf parsley, to serve

tempeh bacon bits

300g tempeh

2 tbsp pure maple syrup

2 tsp smoked paprika

2 tsp tamari

2 tbsp extra virgin olive oil

1 To make the tempeh bacon bits, crumble the tempeh into tiny pieces. Working in 2 batches, place in a doubled piece of kitchen paper; squeeze tightly to remove excess moisture. Whisk together the maple syrup, smoked paprika, and tamari in a small bowl. Heat the olive oil in a non-stick frying pan over a medium heat; cook the tempeh, stirring, for 8 minutes, breaking it up further with a wooden spoon, or until lightly browned and very dry. Add the smoked paprika mixture; cook for a further 10 minutes or until dark, dry, and crumbly. Drain on kitchen paper; season with salt and pepper to taste. Allow to cool.

2 Cook the macaroni in a large saucepan of boiling salted water for 8 minutes or until almost tender; drain. Return the macaroni to the pan.

3 Meanwhile, heat the vegan margarine in a medium saucepan over a high heat. Add the flour, smoked paprika, cayenne pepper, and garlic powder; cook, stirring, for 2 minutes or until smooth and combined. Gradually add the macadamia milk, stirring continuously, until the mixture boils and thickens. Stir in the vegan cheeses and nutritional yeast flakes until the cheeses melt; season with salt and pepper to taste.

4 Stir the hot cheese sauce into the hot macaroni until combined. Spoon the macaroni mixture into 4 serving bowls. Serve topped with tempeh bacon bits and a sprinkling of chives.

TIPS

• Macadamia milk has a smoother, creamier texture and taste than other dairy-free milks.
• The tempeh bacon bits will keep refrigerated for up to 1 week. Scatter over baked sweet potatoes or salads for texture and flavour.

Popcorn cauliflower with spicy tomato sauce

PREP + COOK TIME **1 HOUR** | SERVES **4**

Prep the spicy tomato sauce the day before to fast-track the recipe for family movie night
or when you are binge-watching your favourite TV programmes.

2 tbsp flaxseed meal

1/4 cup (70g) Dijon mustard

2 tbsp hot sauce (see tip)

1²/3 cups (250g) plain flour

2 tsp onion powder

2 tsp garlic powder

2 tsp smoked paprika

1/2 tsp cayenne pepper

1/2 tsp ground white pepper

1 cauliflower (1.5kg)

vegetable oil for deep-frying

sea salt flakes

lemon wedges, to serve

spicy tomato sauce

2 tbsp vegetable oil

2 tsp brown mustard seeds

1 onion (150g), finely chopped

2 garlic cloves, sliced

1 tsp ground ginger

1/2 tsp cayenne pepper

1 tsp freshly ground black pepper

400g can crushed tomatoes

1/3 cup (80ml) malt vinegar

1/4 cup (60ml) pure maple syrup

1 To make the spicy tomato sauce, heat the vegetable oil in a saucepan over a medium heat; cook the mustard seeds for 30 seconds or until they pop. Add the onion, garlic, ginger, cayenne pepper, and black pepper; cook, stirring, for 5 minutes or until the onion softens. Add the tomatoes, malt vinegar, maple syrup, and 1/2 cup (125ml) water; bring to a simmer. Reduce the heat to low; cook for 25 minutes or until reduced and thickened. Allow to cool.

2 Combine the flaxseed meal with 2/3 cup (170ml) water in a large bowl; allow to stand for 5 minutes or until thickened. Add the Dijon mustard and hot sauce; stir to combine. In a second large bowl, combine the flour, onion and garlic powders, smoked paprika, cayenne pepper, and white pepper; season with salt to taste.

3 Cut the cauliflower into 2.5cm florets.

4 Fill a large saucepan one-third full with vegetable oil; heat to 180°C/350°F (or until a cube of bread dropped into the hot oil turns golden in 15 seconds). Add the cauliflower to the flaxseed mixture; stir to coat. Working in batches, toss the cauliflower in the flour mixture to coat. Carefully lower the coated cauliflower into the hot oil; fry for 2 minutes or until golden. Drain on kitchen paper. Season with salt to taste.

5 Serve the cauliflower with the spicy tomato sauce and lemon wedges for squeezing over.

TIP

Use whatever hot sauce you have on hand, such as sriracha or a Mexican hot sauce.

Spicy black bean and avocado nachos

PREP + COOK TIME **30 MINUTES** | SERVES **2**

Take your taste buds to Mexico with these loaded vegan nachos topped with avocado
and a fresh tomato salsa in the style of pico de gallo. You could also make the nachos with
purple-hued beetroot tortilla chips and kidney beans instead of the black beans, if you like.

125g tortilla chips

1/2 cup (60g) Cheddar-style vegan cheese

1/4 tsp cumin seeds

2 tsp extra virgin olive oil

1 small red onion (100g), finely chopped

1 garlic clove, crushed

2 tsp Tabasco pepper sauce (see tip)

2 tbsp tomato purée

400g can black beans, drained, rinsed

1 tomato (150g), finely chopped

1 long red chilli, thinly sliced

1 cup (30g) coriander leaves

1 tbsp freshly squeezed lime juice

1 avocado (250g)

salt and freshly ground black pepper

lime wedges, to serve

1 Preheat the oven to 180°C (160°C fan/350°F/Gas 4). Line a baking tray with baking parchment.

2 Place the tortilla chips on the baking tray, arranging them in an even layer towards its outer edge; scatter over the vegan cheese. Bake for 8 minutes or until the cheese melts and the chips are heated through.

3 Meanwhile, heat a medium frying pan over a medium heat. Add the cumin seeds; stir for 2 minutes or until fragrant. Add the olive oil, onion and garlic; cook, stirring, for 5 minutes or until the onion is soft. Add the Tabasco pepper sauce and tomato purée; cook, stirring, for 1 minute. Next, add the black beans and 1/3 cup (80ml) water; cook, stirring, for 2 minutes or until slightly thickened. Lightly mash some of the beans in the pan using a fork or potato masher.

4 Combine the tomato, chilli, coriander, and lime juice in a small bowl. Season with salt and pepper to taste.

5 Spoon the black bean mixture over the tortilla chips. Cut the avocado into slices. Top the nachos with the avocado slices and tomato salsa. Serve with lime wedges for squeezing over.

TIP

Use whatever hot sauce you have on hand, such as a smoky chipotle or sriracha.

Potato bake with thyme

PREP + COOK TIME **2 HOURS** | SERVES **4**

Dutch cream potatoes are a versatile waxy potato variety with a delicious buttery cream taste that works particularly well in this hearty, comforting dish. The nutritional yeast flakes work double duty, upping the flavour factor and essential B vitamins.

2 tbsp vegan margarine

2 tbsp plain flour

$1/2$ tsp ground nutmeg

1 litre (4 cups) almond milk

2 tbsp nutritional yeast flakes

1.2kg Dutch cream potatoes, peeled, thinly sliced

$1/2$ cup (80g) blanched almonds, coarsely chopped

$1/4$ tsp sweet paprika

2 tbsp fresh thyme leaves

salt and freshly ground black pepper

1 Preheat the oven to 180°C (160°C fan/350°F/Gas 4).

2 Heat the margarine in a medium saucepan over a medium heat until melted. Add the flour and nutmeg; cook, stirring, for 2 minutes. Reduce the heat to low. Gradually add the almond milk, stirring continuously until smooth. Stir in the nutritional yeast flakes. Increase the heat to medium; cook, stirring, for 10 minutes or until the sauce comes to a simmer. Remove from the heat; season with salt and pepper to taste.

3 Grease a 3-litre (12-cup) ovenproof dish. Layer the potatoes in the dish. Pour the white sauce over the potatoes.

4 Cover the dish with foil; bake for 40 minutes. Remove the foil; bake, uncovered, for another 40 minutes. Sprinkle with the almonds and paprika. Return to the oven; bake for a further 10 minutes or until the potatoes are golden.

5 Scatter the potato bake with the thyme; allow to stand for 10 minutes before serving.

TIPS

- You can use orange sweet potatoes instead of potatoes, but you will need to reduce the cooking time accordingly.
- If you like, add breadcrumbs at the same time as sprinkling over the almonds, for extra crunch on top.

Turmeric dosa with masala cauliflower

PREP + COOK TIME **55 MINUTES + OVERNIGHT STANDING** | SERVES **4**

Dosa, a South Indian speciality, are made from a fermented batter of rice and pulses. Serve with lime wedges, green chilli, and curry leaves briefly fried in a little hot oil, if you like.

You will need to start this recipe a day ahead

1 cup (195g) white long-grain rice

1/3 cup (65g) black lentils (urad dal)

2 tbsp yellow split peas

2 tsp sea salt flakes

1/2 tsp caster sugar

1 tsp ground cumin

1/2 tsp ground turmeric

1/3 cup (80ml) olive oil

fresh mint chutney

4 cups (80g) mint leaves

2 garlic cloves

2 tbsp grated fresh root ginger

3 soft fresh dates (60g), pitted

1 long green chilli, coarsely chopped

1/3 cup (80ml) freshly squeezed lime juice

1/4 cup (60ml) extra virgin olive oil

masala cauliflower

1 cauliflower (1.5kg), cut into small florets

1/3 cup (80ml) olive oil

1 red onion (170g), thinly sliced

1 tsp yellow mustard seeds

1 tsp ground turmeric

1/3 cup (3g) fresh curry leaves

1 long green chilli, thinly sliced

1 tbsp grated fresh root ginger

1 To start making the dosas, the day before, rinse the rice, lentils, and split peas in a sieve under cold running water until the water runs clear; put in a large bowl. Cover generously with water; allow to stand, covered, at room temperature overnight.

2 Strain the rice mixture through a fine sieve. Put the mixture in a food processor with 1 1/4 cups (310ml) water; process until it forms a slightly thick, grainy batter. Transfer to a large bowl. Allow to stand, covered, at room temperature for 4 hours to ferment.

3 Start making the mint chutney and masala cauliflower 30 minutes before serving. To make the mint chutney, process the ingredients to a pesto-like consistency.

4 To make the masala cauliflower, blanch the cauliflower in a large saucepan of boiling water for 3 minutes or until just tender. Drain very well. Heat the olive oil in a large frying pan over a medium-high heat; cook the onion, stirring, for 5 minutes or until soft. Add the mustard seeds; cook, stirring, for 1 minute or until the seeds start to pop. Add the turmeric, curry leaves, green chilli, and ginger; cook, stirring, for 1 minute or until fragrant. Add 2 tablespoons water; stir until combined. Add the drained cauliflower, stir until heated through.

5 Stir the sea salt, caster sugar, and spices into the fermented dosa batter. If the batter is too thick, add a little extra water.

6 Heat a 15cm non-stick frying pan over a medium-high heat. Brush the pan lightly with olive oil. Pour 1/3 cup (80ml) batter into the centre of the pan. Immediately, and in a circular motion, spread the batter from the centre towards the edge of the pan, creating a thin pancake. Drizzle 1 teaspoon of the olive oil around the edges and on the surface of the dosa; cook for 3 minutes or until golden and crisp. Slide a spatula around the edges of the dosa and fold in half; slide onto a plate. Repeat with the remaining batter and olive oil to make 12 dosas in total.

7 Fill the dosas with the masala cauliflower; serve with the mint chutney.

Lentil loaf with maple glaze

PREP + COOK TIME **1 HOUR 30 MINUTES** | SERVES **8**

For a shared lunch or light supper, serve this thyme-infused loaf as part of a ploughman's platter with pickled vegetables, beetroot dip, marinated olives, and cornichons. And you can use the leftovers, should there be any, for a sandwich filling with lettuce and tomato.

1 cup (200g) green lentils, rinsed

1/2 cup (100g) brown rice

3 cups (750ml) vegetable stock

1 cup (100g) walnuts

1 tbsp extra virgin olive oil, plus extra for greasing

1 small red onion (100g), finely diced

2 trimmed celery sticks (200g), finely diced

1 garlic clove, crushed

1 small apple (130g), finely grated

1/4 cup (40g) flaxseed meal

3/4 cup (90g) quick oats

1/3 cup (8g) thyme leaves, plus extra sprigs, to serve (optional)

1/3 cup (95g) tomato ketchup

2 tbsp pure maple syrup

2 tbsp balsamic vinegar

salt and freshly ground black pepper

1 Preheat the oven to 200°C (180°C fan/400°F/Gas 6). Oil a 12cm x 25cm loaf tin; line with baking parchment.

2 Put the green lentils, brown rice, and vegetable stock in a medium saucepan; bring to the boil. Reduce the heat to medium; simmer gently for 40 minutes or until the lentils and rice are tender and the stock has been absorbed.

3 Meanwhile, put the walnuts on a baking tray; toast for 4 minutes or until golden. Allow to cool, then coarsely chop. Reduce the oven temperature to 160°C (140°C fan/325°F/Gas 3).

4 Heat the olive oil in a medium frying pan; cook the onion and celery, stirring, for 3 minutes or until soft. Add the garlic and apple; cook for 5 minutes. Remove from the heat.

5 Transfer the lentil mixture to a large bowl; add the walnuts and the onion-celery mixture.

6 Combine the flaxseed meal with 1/2 cup (125ml) water in a small bowl until it becomes gel-like in consistency. Add to the lentil mixture with the quick oats and the 1/3 cup (8g) thyme leaves. Season with salt and pepper to taste. Stir well to combine. Spoon the mixture into the prepared loaf tin; smooth the surface.

7 Whisk together the tomato ketchup, maple syrup, and balsamic vinegar in a small bowl. Brush half of the glaze mixture over the top of the loaf. Cover with foil.

8 Bake the loaf for 40 minutes. Remove the foil; brush with the remaining glaze. Bake for a further 20 minutes or until the top is browned. Transfer the tin to a wire rack, and allow the loaf to cool completely before slicing. Serve topped with extra sprigs of thyme, if you like.

TIP

A great vegan alternative to meatloaf, the loaf can be served warm, loaded with mashed potato, steamed vegetables, and a vegan gravy, if you like.

The botanist burger

PREP + COOK TIME **50 MINUTES + REFRIGERATION** | MAKES **4**

Here it is. Definitive proof that a fabulous vegan burger, sauce, and 'crisps' really can be constructed solely from plant-based food.

800g canned chickpeas, drained, rinsed (see tips)

2 tbsp chickpea flour (besan)

²/₃ cup (15g) firmly packed flat-leaf parsley leaves

1 cup (25g) firmly packed mint leaves

2 tsp finely grated lemon zest

6 spring onions, finely chopped

¹/₂ cup (125g) vegan mayonnaise
(use Everyday Mayo on page 55 or buy ready-made)

2 garlic cloves, crushed

2 tbsp finely chopped chives

2 courgettes (240g), thinly sliced lengthways

2 tbsp extra virgin olive oil

4 seeded sourdough bread rolls, halved

2 small avocados (400g), sliced

2 cups (80g) firmly packed watercress leaves

salt and freshly ground black pepper

kale crisps

250g kale

1 tbsp extra virgin olive oil

sea salt flakes

TIPS

• Save the drained liquid, called aquafaba, from the canned chickpeas to make vegan meringue (see page 158) or for the Everyday Mayo on page 55. Store aquafaba in a container in the fridge for up to 2 days or freeze for up to 3 months.

• The patties can be made a day ahead; keep in the fridge, covered, until needed. Or, freeze in an airtight container, individually wrapped, for up to 2 months.

1 Preheat the oven to 180°C (160°C fan/350°F/Gas 4). Line 2 baking trays with baking parchment.

2 Make the kale chips. Remove the stems from the kale; tear the leaves into medium-sized pieces. Put in a large bowl with oil. Massage the olive oil into the kale leaves, then arrange them in a single layer on the prepared trays. Bake for 10 minutes. Rotate the trays; bake for a further 5 minutes or until the kale is crisp. Allow to cool. Season with salt flakes.

3 Meanwhile, process the chickpeas, chickpea flour, parsley, mint, and lemon zest until the mixture comes together. Transfer to a medium bowl; stir in the spring onions; season with salt and pepper to taste. Shape the mixture into 4 patties. Place on a plate; refrigerate for 20 minutes.

4 Process the vegan mayonnaise, garlic, and chives in a clean food processor bowl until combined. Set aside.

5 Heat a ridged cast-iron grill pan until hot. Chargrill the courgettes over a medium-high heat for 2 minutes on each side or until tender. Transfer to a plate; cover to keep warm.

6 Brush 1 tablespoon of the olive oil on the same cast-iron grill pan, then cook the patties for 2 minutes on each side or until browned and heated through.

7 Brush the insides of each roll with the remaining olive oil, and lightly toast the cut sides on the cast-iron grill pan.

8 Spoon the mayonnaise mixture onto the bottom half of each roll; top with the chickpea patties and courgettes. Slice the avocado and arrange over the courgettes, then top with the watercress. Sandwich each roll with its top half. Serve with the kale chips.

Daily greens skillet filo pie

PREP + COOK TIME **50 MINUTES + COOLING** | SERVES **4**

Eat a broader diet by rotating the types of greens you eat – such as in this pie – to capture the different valuable nutritional qualities each provides. Serve the pie with dairy-free yogurt or a beetroot hummus, or try it with the Beetroot and Za'atar Dip on page 76, if you like.

750g Swiss or rainbow chard

1/4 cup (60ml) extra virgin olive oil

1 leek (350g), thinly sliced

3 garlic cloves, crushed

1 tbsp white spelt flour

1 cup (250ml) vegetable stock

2 courgettes (240g), cut into 1cm slices

200g broccolini (Tenderstem broccoli), cut into 5cm lengths

1 cup (120g) frozen baby peas

6 sheets of filo pastry

2 tsp black sesame seeds

2 tsp white sesame seeds

salt and freshly ground black pepper

lemon cheeks, to serve

1 Preheat the oven to 220°C (200°C fan/425°F/Gas 7).

2 Trim the ends of the chard stems; chop the stems into 1cm pieces. Coarsely shred the leaves.

3 Heat 2 tablespoons of the olive oil in a 26cm (base measurement), 27cm (top measurement) ovenproof frying pan over a medium heat. Cook the leek and chard stems, stirring occasionally, for 7 minutes or until softened. Add the garlic; cook, stirring, for 1 minute or until fragrant. Add the spelt flour; stir until combined. Gradually stir in the vegetable stock; bring to the boil. Simmer, uncovered, for 2 minutes or until the liquid has slightly thickened.

4 Pour boiling water over the shredded chard leaves in a large heatproof bowl; allow to stand for 1 minute, then drain. Refresh in another bowl of iced water; drain. Squeeze out as much liquid as possible, then stir into the leek mixture (still in the pan) with the courgettes, broccolini, and baby peas. Season with salt and pepper to taste. Allow to cool for 20 minutes.

5 Brush the filo sheets with the remaining olive oil. Loosely scrunch the pastry sheets over the chard mixture in the pan; sprinkle with the black and white sesame seeds. Bake for 15 minutes or until the pastry is golden. Allow the pie to stand for 10 minutes before serving.

TIPS

- This pie can be eaten hot, warm, or cold. To take on a picnic, simply cool, wrap the frying pan in a clean tea towel, and away you go!
- Make sure the pan you use is non-reactive – that is, not aluminium, pitted, or with any rust spots – to avoid the greens being tainted by a metallic taste.

Veggie patties with beetroot and caraway chutney

PREP + COOK TIME **1 HOUR + COOLING + REFRIGERATION** | MAKES **6**

These patties are based on millet, rather than lentils. This mild-flavoured, starchy whole grain is rich in carbohydrates, but also contains more calcium than other cereal grains.

³/₄ cup (150g) millet

¹/₄ cup (60ml) extra virgin olive oil

1 small onion (80g), finely chopped

1 garlic clove, crushed

2cm piece of fresh root ginger (10g), grated

1 small orange sweet potato (250g), peeled, grated

1 cup (160g) frozen sweetcorn kernels

75g baby spinach leaves

¹/₄ cup (15g) chopped basil leaves

³/₄ cup (210g) hulled tahini

¹/₂ cup (60g) ground almonds

grapeseed oil for shallow-frying

6 wholegrain bread rolls

100g mixed salad leaves

¹/₂ cup (120g) vegan cashew nut cheese

salt and freshly ground black pepper

beetroot and caraway chutney

1 tbsp extra virgin olive oil

1 red onion (150g), finely chopped

2 tsp caraway seeds

2 beetroot (400g), coarsely grated

¹/₂ cup (125ml) apple cider vinegar

³/₄ cup (165g) raw sugar

³/₄ cup (180ml) coconut water

1 Make the beetroot and caraway chutney. Heat the olive oil in a medium saucepan over a medium heat; cook the onion and caraway seeds, stirring, for 5 minutes or until the onion softens. Add the beetroot, cider vinegar, raw sugar, and coconut water; bring to a simmer. Simmer, uncovered, over a low-medium heat, for 45 minutes or until the beetroot is soft and the mixture is thickened. Season with salt and pepper to taste. Allow to cool.

2 Meanwhile, bring the millet and 3 cups (750ml) water to the boil in a medium saucepan. Reduce the heat to medium; simmer, uncovered, for 15 minutes or until soft. Drain.

3 Heat the olive oil in a large frying pan over a medium heat; cook the onion, garlic, and ginger, stirring, for 5 minutes or until the onion softens. Add the sweet potato and sweetcorn; cook, stirring, for 5 minutes or until the sweetcorn softens. Remove from the heat; stir in the spinach. Transfer to a medium bowl; stir in the cooked millet, basil, hulled tahini, and ground almonds. Season with salt and pepper to taste.

4 Shape the mixture into 12 patties; place on a baking tray lined with baking parchment. Refrigerate for 30 minutes.

5 Heat enough grapeseed oil for shallow-frying in a large frying pan over a medium-high heat. Shallow-fry the patties, in batches, for 3 minutes on each side or until golden. Drain the patties on kitchen paper.

6 Serve the veggie patties on the bread rolls with the salad leaves, cashew nut cheese, and beetroot and caraway chutney.

TIP

The beetroot chutney can be made up to a week ahead. Store in an airtight container in the fridge.

Mushroom congee

PREP + COOK TIME **55 MINUTES** | SERVES **6**

In China and Southeast Asia, congee is seen as the ultimate comfort food. Rich in B vitamins and minerals such as zinc and selenium, here shiitake mushrooms add their own comfort.

2 cups (500ml) groundnut oil

200g shiitake mushrooms, stalks removed, 4 whole and the rest sliced

12cm piece of fresh root ginger, thinly sliced

1 cup (215g) sushi rice

2 litres (8 cups) salt-reduced vegetable stock

200g enoki mushrooms, stalks trimmed

6 shallots (150g), thinly sliced

6 large garlic cloves, thinly sliced

2 spring onions, thinly sliced

1/2 cup (15g) loosely packed coriander leaves

1/4 cup (70g) Thai chilli jam

2 tsp tamari

2 tsp sesame oil

1 Heat 2 tablespoons of the groundnut oil in a large wok over a high heat; stir-fry the whole shiitake mushrooms for 4 minutes or until tender; set aside. Stir-fry the sliced shiitake mushrooms and ginger for 4 minutes. Add the rice; stir-fry for a further 2 minutes. Add the vegetable stock and 2 cups (500ml) water; cover the wok, bring to the boil. Uncover; reduce the heat. Simmer, uncovered, for 40 minutes or until the congee is thick like porridge, stirring frequently to avoid it catching on the bottom. Using a spoon, skim off and discard any foam from the top during cooking.

2 Meanwhile, heat the remaining oil in a small saucepan to 180°C/350°F (or until a cube of bread dropped into the hot oil turns golden brown in 15 seconds). Fry the enoki mushrooms for 40 seconds or until golden and crisp. Remove from the pan with a slotted spoon; drain on kitchen paper. Fry the shallots for 2 minutes or until golden and crisp. Remove from the pan with a slotted spoon; drain on kitchen paper. Fry the garlic for 30 seconds or until just golden. Remove from the pan with a slotted spoon; drain on kitchen paper. (Be careful not to cook the garlic for too long; otherwise it will become bitter.) In a small bowl, gently toss the cooled enoki, shallot, and garlic with the spring onion and coriander.

3 Combine the chilli jam with 1/4 cup (60ml) water in a small bowl.

4 Serve the congee in bowls, drizzled with the chilli jam, tamari, and sesame oil. Top with the whole shiitake mushrooms and fried enoki mixture. Serve immediately.

TIPS

- You can buy fried shallots and garlic from Asian supermarkets or grocers to save time.
- Substitute chestnut mushrooms for the shiitake mushrooms, if you like.
- If you have leftover congee, keep refrigerated in an airtight container, separate from the garnishes, for up to 2 days. Reheat with some hot water to adjust the consistency.
- Serve topped with chopped roasted peanuts or cashews for extra protein, if you like.

Hoisin baked aubergine with steamed greens

PREP + COOK TIME **40 MINUTES** | SERVES **4**

Use your favourite greens in this recipe – broccoli, choi sum (Chinese flowering cabbage), gai lan (Chinese broccoli), asparagus, and green or snake beans would all work well. Be careful not to overcook them, as you want them to hold their shape and keep their vibrant colour.

2 aubergines (600g), thickly sliced

1 cup (280g) hoisin sauce

1 tbsp white sesame seeds

2 tsp black sesame seeds

270g buckwheat soba noodles (see tip)

1/2 cup (125ml) tamari

2 tbsp soft brown sugar

1 tbsp sesame oil

175g broccolini (Tenderstem broccoli)

1 baby pak choi (150g)

thinly sliced spring onion, to serve

1 Preheat the oven to 180°C (160°C fan/350°F/Gas 4). Line 2 baking trays with baking parchment.

2 Arrange the aubergines on the prepared trays in a single layer; brush both sides with the hoisin sauce. Sprinkle with the white and black sesame seeds. Bake the aubergines for 20 minutes or until tender.

3 Meanwhile, cook the noodles in a large saucepan of boiling salted water for 3 minutes or until just tender. Drain; cover to keep warm.

4 To make the dressing, whisk together the tamari, soft brown sugar, and sesame oil in a small bowl. Put the noodles and half of the dressing in a large bowl; toss to combine.

5 Boil, steam, or microwave the broccolini and pak choi until tender; drain.

6 Serve the aubergines with the noodles, greens, and remaining dressing. Top with thinly sliced spring onion, if you like.

TIP

Take care not to overcook the soba noodles, as they will continue to cook once drained.

Shepherdless pie

PREP + COOK TIME **1 HOUR** | SERVES **4**

Who needs lamb when you have lentils, mushrooms, a rainbow of other tasty vegetables, and a pillowy polenta crust? This vegan twist on the classic shepherd's pie is just as hearty as the original and oh-so-tasty!

1 cup (200g) French-style green lentils

2 tbsp extra virgin olive oil

1 onion (150g), coarsely chopped

2 garlic cloves, crushed

2 tsp fennel seeds

1 carrot (120g), coarsely chopped

200g chestnut mushrooms, halved

400g grape tomatoes

2 tbsp tomato purée

1 cup (250ml) vegetable stock

60g baby spinach

salt and freshly ground black pepper

polenta topping

1 litre (4 cups) vegetable stock

1 cup (170g) polenta

2 tbsp finely chopped fresh thyme leaves, plus extra sprigs, to serve

2 tbsp olive oil

2 tbsp nutritional yeast flakes

1 Cook the lentils in a medium saucepan of boiling water, uncovered, for 12 minutes or until just tender; drain.

2 Meanwhile, heat the olive oil in a large, deep frying pan over a medium-high heat. Cook the onion, garlic, and fennel seeds, stirring, for 5 minutes or until the onion is soft. Add the carrot, mushrooms, and tomatoes; cook, covered, for 10 minutes or until the carrot softens. Stir in the tomato purée; cook for 1 minute. Add the vegetable stock; bring to the boil. Cook, uncovered, for 3 minutes or until slightly thickened. Stir in the lentils and spinach; season with salt and pepper to taste. Cover to keep warm.

3 To make the polenta topping, bring the vegetable stock to the boil in a large saucepan. Gradually add the polenta and the 2 tablespoons chopped thyme to the stock, stirring constantly. Reduce the heat; cook, stirring, for 10 minutes or until the polenta thickens. Stir in the olive oil and nutritional yeast flakes. Season with salt and pepper to taste.

4 Preheat the grill to a high heat. Put the lentil mixture in a 2-litre (8-cup) ovenproof dish; spread with the polenta topping. Grill for 15 minutes or until golden and crisp (be careful not to let the topping scorch).

5 Serve the pie topped with extra thyme leaves; season with salt and pepper to taste.

TIPS

- French-style green lentils are related to the famed French lentils du Puy; these tiny green-blue lentils have a nutty, earthy flavour and a hardy nature that allows them to be rapidly cooked without disintegrating.
- Use a mixture of Puy and green lentils, if you like.

SWEET TREATS

Whatever and whenever the occasion, there is something here to soothe your craving, from impressive cakes and tempting biscuits to vegan ice cream and summery tarts.

Citrus poppyseed celebration cake

PREP + COOK TIME **1 HOUR 30 MINUTES + STANDING, COOLING + REFRIGERATION** | SERVES **12**

Hosting a birthday, afternoon tea, Mother's Day, or other celebration? This cake ticks all the boxes for when you need a spectacularly delicious cake with a visual appeal all its own. Serve topped with seasonal fruit, thin strips of citrus zest, and edible flowers for extra oomph.

1 cup (250ml) orange juice

1/3 cup (50g) poppy seeds

2 cups (500ml) canned coconut milk

1½ tbsp apple cider vinegar

2½ cups (375g) self-raising flour

2 tsp bicarbonate of soda

2 tsp baking powder

1⅓ cups (300g) golden caster sugar

2 tbsp finely grated orange zest

750g dairy-free coconut yogurt (use Home-made Coconut Yogurt on page 21 or buy ready-made)

250g blueberries

3 tsp finely grated lemon zest

1 cup (160g) vegan icing sugar

1½ tbsp lemon juice

unsprayed edible flowers (optional)

TIPS

• The cakes can be made a day ahead to the end of step 6; store in an airtight container at room temperature. They can also be frozen for up to 3 months. Allow to thaw when needed, then continue with the recipe.

• To make in 3 layers, simply prep three 20cm or 23cm cake tins and divide the cake mixture evenly among them. Use a set of scales for equal portions. Adjust your baking time to 35–40 minutes.

• Keep any leftovers refrigerated until eating.

1 Preheat the oven to 170°C (150°C fan/340°F/Gas 4). Grease two deep 20cm round cake tins; line the bottoms and sides with baking parchment.

2 Combine the orange juice and poppy seeds in a small bowl; allow to stand for 15 minutes.

3 Meanwhile, combine the coconut milk and apple cider vinegar in a medium bowl; allow to stand for 5 minutes.

4 Sift the flour, bicarbonate of soda, baking powder, and caster sugar into a large bowl. Make a well in the centre. Add the seed mixture, coconut milk mixture, and orange zest; whisk until just combined. Divide the mixture evenly between the prepared tins.

5 Bake the cakes for 50 minutes or until a skewer inserted into the centre comes out clean. Allow the cakes to cool in the tins for 10 minutes, before turning out onto wire racks to cool completely.

6 Split the cakes in half horizontally; refrigerate for 2 hours.

7 For best results, start the final assembly of the cake shortly before you are ready to serve. Place one base layer of cake on a plate. Top with a quarter each of the coconut yogurt, blueberries, and lemon zest. Repeat the layering with the remaining cake layers, yogurt, blueberries, and lemon zest, finishing with the final cake layer, topped with yogurt.

8 Sift the icing sugar into a medium bowl; stir in the lemon juice until smooth and the glaze is your desired thickness. Drizzle the glaze over the top of the cake. Top with edible flowers, if you like.

Spiced banana bread

PREP + COOK TIME **1 HOUR 15 MINUTES + COOLING** | SERVES **10 SLICES**

Naturally sweet and fruity, banana bread is easy to make and a tempting treat for an afternoon snack or even breakfast. For a really good banana taste, you will need 2 large overripe bananas (460g) for the bread, plus the 2 smaller just-ripe bananas to top the loaf.

1¹/₄ cups (185g) self-raising flour

1 cup (130g) white spelt flour

1 tsp baking powder

2 tsp ground cinnamon

1 tsp ground cardamom

1 tsp ground ginger

1 tsp vanilla powder

1 tbsp white chia seeds

³/₄ cup (75g) walnuts, coarsely chopped

1 cup (240g) mashed overripe bananas, plus extra
2 just-ripe small bananas (260g), sliced lengthways

³/₄ cup (180ml) almond milk

¹/₃ cup (70g) coconut oil, melted

2 tbsp pure maple syrup, plus extra, to serve (optional)

¹/₃ cup (90g) cashew cream or dairy-free coconut yogurt (use Home-made Coconut Yogurt on page 21 or buy ready-made)

unsprayed edible flowers (optional)

1 Preheat the oven to 180°C (160°C/350°F/Gas 4). Grease a 19cm x 9cm x 7cm loaf tin with cooking spray; line with baking parchment, leaving 5cm hanging over the sides.

2 Sift the flours, baking powder, spices, and vanilla powder into a large bowl; stir in the chia seeds and ¹/₂ cup (50g) of the walnuts. Make a well in the centre. Add the combined mashed bananas, almond milk, and coconut oil to the dry ingredients; stir until just combined.

3 Spread the mixture into the prepared loaf tin. Top with the remaining ¹/₄ cup (25g) walnuts and the extra sliced bananas. Bake for 50 minutes or until a skewer inserted into the centre comes out clean. Brush the loaf with the 2 tablespoons maple syrup. Allow to cool in the tin for 15 minutes, before turning out onto a wire rack.

4 Serve slices of the banana bread loaf, warm or cooled, with the cashew cream, drizzled with a little extra maple syrup and topped with edible flowers, if you like.

TIPS

- For best results, it's important that the bananas used in the loaf are overripe.
- Cashew cream is available from health food shops.
- Loaves tend to crack because of the small surface area. To test whether a loaf is cooked, insert the skewer as close to the centre as possible, but not through a crack; inserting the skewer through a crack will give an inaccurate result.

Blueberry coconut bars

PREP + COOK TIME **45 MINUTES + FREEZING** | MAKES **12**

Make your own coconut and dark vegan chocolate treats at home. These sinful but divine blueberry-flavoured bars are best served at room temperature, when the filling will be soft and moist – it will be difficult to stop at just one!

2½ cups (200g) desiccated coconut

80g coconut butter, melted

2 tbsp coconut oil, melted

¼ cup (18g) freeze-dried blueberry powder (see tips)

⅓ cup (80ml) coconut cream

2 tbsp pure maple syrup

chocolate coating

120g cacao butter, finely chopped

½ cup (115g) coconut oil

¼ cup (60ml) pure maple syrup

½ tsp vanilla extract

1 cup (100g) cacao powder

to decorate

1 tbsp desiccated coconut

½ tsp freeze-dried blueberry powder

fresh blueberries

edible dried rose petals (optional)

TIPS

- Freeze-dried blueberry powder is available from health food shops, specialist grocers, and online.
- If the chocolate coating thickens, place the bowl over hot water until melted.
- The bars will keep, stored in an airtight container in the freezer, for up to 1 month. Remove from the freezer 45 minutes before eating, to allow time to thaw and soften.

1 Grease a 12cm x 25cm (base measurement) and 15cm x 27cm (top measurement) loaf tin; line with cling film, allowing excess to overhang the sides of the tin.

2 Put the desiccated coconut in a medium bowl. Using your fingertips, rub in the melted coconut butter and coconut oil until the mixture resembles breadcrumbs. Mix in the blueberry powder, then the coconut cream and maple syrup. Evenly press the mixture into the prepared loaf tin; freeze for 30 minutes or until firm.

3 Remove the mixture from the tin; trim the edges and cut crossways into 12 bars. (If you like, round the corners of each bar using your hand and/or a palette knife.) Place the bars on a baking tray lined with baking parchment; freeze while making the chocolate coating.

4 To make the chocolate coating, put the cacao butter, coconut oil, maple syrup, and vanilla extract in a medium heatproof bowl over a smaller heatproof bowl of boiling water; whisk until combined. Whisk in the cacao powder until combined and smooth.

5 Working with one bar at a time, dip the bars in the chocolate coating, holding the bars underneath with 2 forks. Gently shake off any excess chocolate and return the bars to the tray. Freeze for 10 minutes until set.

6 Trim off any excess chocolate; double-dip the bars using the leftover chocolate. Return to the freezer to set for 10 minutes, and trim again.

7 To decorate, combine the coconut and blueberry powder in a small bowl, and sprinkle over the bars in a line. Decorate with fresh blueberries and dried rose petals, if you like.

Strawberries-and-cream vegan cheesecake

PREP TIME **1 HOUR 10 MINUTES + STANDING + REFRIGERATION** | SERVES **16**

Pretty as a picture, this dreamy, creamy no-bake cheesecake is simply delectable. Just remember that you need to start this recipe at least a day ahead, to allow time for it to set.

You will need to start this recipe at least a day ahead

2¹/₂ cups (375g) raw cashews

1 cup (140g) raw macadamias

³/₄ cup (60g) desiccated coconut

¹/₂ cup (60g) ground almonds

6 soft fresh dates (120g), pitted

³/₄ tsp vanilla bean paste

³/₄ cup (150g) coconut oil, melted

400g small strawberries, plus extra, halved, to serve

1 cup (240g) dairy-free coconut yogurt (use Home-made Coconut Yogurt on page 21 or buy ready-made)

¹/₂ cup (125ml) light agave syrup

1 tbsp finely grated lemon zest

¹/₃ cup (80ml) lemon juice

80g cacao butter, melted

coconut flakes and unsprayed edible flowers, to serve (optional)

TIPS

- If you have one, use a high-powered blender in steps 5 and 6, to achieve a really smooth result.
- The cheesecake will keep in an airtight container in the fridge for up to 4 days.

1 Put the cashews in a medium bowl with enough cold water to cover. Allow to stand, covered, for 4 hours. Drain, then rinse under cold water. Drain well a second time.

2 Grease a 23cm round springform cake tin. Line the bottom and side of the tin with baking parchment, extending the parchment 5cm above the top edge of the tin.

3 Process the macadamias, desiccated coconut, ground almonds, dates, and ¹/₄ teaspoon of the vanilla bean paste until the mixture resembles coarse crumbs. Add 1 tablespoon of the coconut oil; process until combined and the mixture starts to stick together. Press the mixture over the bottom of the prepared tin. Next, using the back of a spoon, press down firmly and level the mixture to form the cheesecake base.

4 Hull then thinly slice the 400g small strawberries lengthways. The strawberries shouldn't be more than 3.5cm tall, or the tips will not be covered by the filling; trim if needed. Place the tallest strawberry slices around the side of the cake tin, sticking them to the baking parchment; reserve the remaining slices. Refrigerate the tin until needed.

5 Blend the drained cashews with the coconut yogurt, agave syrup, lemon zest, lemon juice, and the remaining ¹/₂ teaspoon vanilla bean paste until as smooth as possible. Add the cacao butter and the remaining coconut oil; blend again until as smooth as possible. Pour two-thirds of the cashew mixture over the cheesecake base; smooth the surface. Refrigerate while preparing the strawberry layer.

6 Blend the reserved strawberry slices until as smooth as possible; stir into the remaining cashew mixture. Gently spoon the strawberry-cashew mixture over the cream layer; do not pour or the layers will combine. Refrigerate overnight or until set.

7 Remove the cheesecake from the tin, and place on a plate to serve. Top with halved extra strawberries, sprinkling with coconut flakes and edible flowers, if you like.

Strawberry mylkshake popsicles

PREP TIME **25 MINUTES + STANDING + FREEZING** | MAKES **8**

Perfect for a sweltering summer's day, these luscious ice lollies are best made
with strawberries at their ripest, with a strong aroma and taste, so that they infuse the
popsicles with the maximum amount of flavour.

You will need to start this recipe a day ahead

$1/4$ cup (40g) raw cashews

$1^2/3$ cups (400ml) coconut cream

$1/4$ cup (60ml) pure maple syrup

1 tsp pure vanilla extract

200g strawberries, hulled

chocolate coating

$1/4$ cup (50g) coconut oil

$1/4$ cup (60g) cacao butter, chopped

2 tbsp pure maple syrup

$1/2$ cup (50g) cacao powder

1 Put the cashews in a medium bowl; cover with cold water. Allow to stand, covered, for 4 hours or overnight. Drain the cashews, then rinse under cold water; drain well.

2 Blend the drained cashews with the coconut cream, maple syrup, vanilla extract, and strawberries until as smooth as possible.

3 Pour the mixture into eight $1/3$-cup (80ml) popsicle moulds; freeze for 1 hour. Insert popsicle sticks; freeze overnight or until firm.

4 Run the moulds quickly under cold water; remove the popsicles. Place the popsicles on a tray lined with baking parchment; return to the freezer with the popsicles still on the tray.

5 Make the chocolate coating. Put the coconut oil and cacao butter in a medium heatproof bowl over a smaller heatproof bowl of boiling water. Whisk until combined and smooth, then whisk in the maple syrup. Whisk in the cacao powder until combined and smooth. Pour the chocolate into a small wide glass; this will make it easier to dip the popsicles.

6 Dip the tips of the popsicles, one at a time, into the chocolate coating. Gently shake off any excess chocolate. Return to the parchment-lined tray; freeze for 5 minutes or until the chocolate is firm. If you want to alternate the chocolate pattern, drizzle some of the popsicles with chocolate (see tips).

TIPS

▪ If you have one, use a high-speed blender in step 2; this type of blender will produce a very smooth consistency.

▪ To create thin drizzled lines of chocolate on the popsicles, use a resealable plastic bag. Spoon the melted chocolate coating into the bag, then cut off a tiny tip at one corner of the bag. Drizzle the chocolate over the popsicles. Freeze for 5 minutes or until set; turn over and repeat.

▪ Store the popsicles in an airtight container, placing a sheet of baking parchment between them. The popsicles can be frozen for up to 2 months.

Popcorn rocky road bark

PREP + COOK TIME **15 MINUTES + FREEZING** | SERVES **8**

Simple to put together and even easier to eat, this no-bake slice fuses two much-loved snack foods into one decadent confection. Coconut oil has a low melting point and the rice malt syrup keeps the bark soft, so you need to eat these treats while they are still frozen.

$^1/_2$ cup (100g) coconut oil

$^1/_2$ cup (50g) cacao powder

$^1/_2$ cup (175g) rice malt syrup

1 tbsp almond butter

2 tsp vanilla extract

1$^1/_2$ cups (25g) salted natural popcorn

1 cup (50g) flaked coconut

$^3/_4$ cup (125g) dry-roasted almonds

$^1/_3$ cup (45g) dried sweetened cranberries

1 Line a 10cm x 20cm loaf tin with baking parchment, extending the parchment 2cm above the top edges of the tin.

2 Melt the coconut oil in a medium saucepan over a low heat. Remove from the heat; whisk in the cacao powder, rice malt syrup, almond butter, and vanilla extract until the cacao is dissolved and the mixture is smooth.

3 Stir in three-quarters each of the popcorn, flaked coconut, almonds, and cranberries. Spoon the mixture into the prepared tin; spread evenly over the bottom. Scatter with the remaining popcorn, flaked coconut, almonds, and cranberries; press lightly into the cocoa mixture to secure.

4 Freeze the bark for 15 minutes or until frozen solid.

5 Cut the frozen bark into slices or chunks. Eat immediately, frozen, or store in an airtight container in the freezer for up to 1 month.

TIP

You can use freeze-dried strawberries or raspberries instead of the cranberries.

Frozen no-bake blueberry meringue slab pie

PREP + COOK TIME **40 MINUTES + FREEZING** | SERVES **8**

Aquafaba, in this case the water drained from a can of chickpeas, is used to make the vegan-friendly meringue topping this dessert. To brown the meringue, you will need a kitchen blowtorch, available from kitchen shops or DIY stores.

1 cup (90g) rolled oats

1 cup (160g) natural almonds, roasted

¾ cup (175g) soft medjool dates

¼ cup (60ml) extra virgin olive oil

1 tbsp pure maple syrup

½ tsp sea salt flakes

2 cups (300g) frozen blueberries

300g silken tofu

270ml can coconut cream

½ cup (120g) barley malt syrup

1 tsp vanilla extract

2 limes (130g), zest cut into strips, juiced

fresh blueberries, to serve (optional)

Italian meringue

1 cup (220g) caster sugar

400g can chickpeas, unopened

2 tsp cream of tartar

TIPS

• Use the chickpeas in recipes such as Avocado Toasts with Smoky Chickpeas (page 40) or Wasabi Edamame Hummus Pack (page 86).

• If you don't have a kitchen blowtorch, place the dessert under a hot grill for 30 seconds or until the meringue is lightly browned.

1 Line a 25cm x 12cm x 8cm loaf tin with 2 layers of baking parchment, extending the papers 5cm over the 2 long sides.

2 Process the rolled oats, almonds, dates, oil, maple syrup, and salt until coarsely combined and sticking together well. Press the mixture evenly and firmly onto the bottom of the lined tin.

3 Put the blueberries, tofu, coconut cream, barley malt syrup, vanilla extract, and ¼ cup (60ml) of the lime juice in a food processor; process until smooth. Pour into the loaf tin; freeze for 2 hours or until set.

4 To make the Italian meringue, put the sugar and ⅓ cup (80ml) water in a small saucepan; stir gently. Place the pan over a medium heat; cook without stirring, for 15 minutes or until the syrup reaches 118°C/244°F on a cooking thermometer.

5 Meanwhile, strain the chickpeas through a sieve set over a small bowl; you should have ¾ cup (180ml) chickpea liquid (aquafaba). Reserve the chickpeas for another use (see tips). Put the aquafaba in the bowl of an electric mixer. Whisk on high speed until tripled in volume, then whisk in the cream of tartar.

6 When the sugar syrup has reached 118°C/244°F, slowly pour into the meringue mixture. Increase the speed to maximum; whisk for a further 3 minutes or until the bowl feels at room temperature when touched.

7 Spoon the Italian meringue over the blueberry layer; using the back of a spoon, swirl the meringue to form peaks. Using a blowtorch, lightly brown the meringue (see tips). Return to the freezer for 30 minutes or until ready to serve.

8 Serve topped with the lime zest and extra fresh blueberries, if you like.

Giant brownie sundae

PREP + COOK TIME **45 MINUTES** | SERVES **4**

What chocolate lover could resist this brownie-meets-sundae extravaganza where everyone can dig in to their heart's content? You can go the whole hog and add all the extras – chocolate sauce, ice cream, and toppings – or keep it simple, if you like.

1 cup (150g) plain flour

1/2 cup (110g) firmly packed soft brown sugar

1/2 cup (110g) caster sugar

1/2 cup (65g) Dutch-process cocoa powder

1/3 cup (80ml) vegetable oil

1 tsp vanilla bean paste

1/2 tsp sea salt flakes

1 tsp baking powder

75g vegan chocolate, chopped

4 scoops of chocolate dairy-free ice cream

15g plain rectangular ice-cream wafers

50g vegan mini chocolate sandwich cookies

8 maraschino cherries with stalks (see tip)

chocolate sauce

1/4 cup (60ml) pure maple syrup

1/2 cup (50g) Dutch-process cocoa powder

1 tbsp coconut oil

1 tsp vanilla bean paste

1 Preheat the oven to 180°C (160°C fan/350°F/Gas 4). Grease a 20cm cast-iron frying pan or round cake tin or pie tin.

2 Put 1/4 cup (35g) of the flour and 1/2 cup (125ml) water in a saucepan over a medium heat; cook, whisking continuously, until the mixture thickens. Transfer to a bowl; allow to cool.

3 In a large bowl, stir the sugars, cocoa powder, 1/3 cup (80ml) vegetable oil, vanilla bean paste, and sea salt into a paste. Add the cooked flour mixture; stir until well combined. Stir in the combined remaining sifted flour and baking powder, followed by the chopped chocolate. (The mixture will be very thick.)

4 Press the brownie mixture into the prepared pan or tin; bake for 20 minutes or until a skewer inserted into the centre comes out clean.

5 Meanwhile, make the chocolate sauce. Put the ingredients in a small saucepan. Add 1/2 cup (125ml) water. Bring to a simmer, whisking occasionally until smooth, for 5 minutes. Allow to cool. (The sauce will thicken on cooling.)

6 Top the brownie with the scoops of chocolate dairy-free ice cream, wafers, mini chocolate sandwich cookies, and maraschino cherries; drizzle with the chocolate sauce. Serve immediately.

TIP

Check the label to ensure the maraschino cherries you choose are suitable for vegans, or use Amarena cherries in syrup instead.

Fruity soft serves

PREP TIME **20 MINUTES + FREEZING** | MAKES **12**

Impress family and friends with these cooling ices on a hot summer's day. They are straightforward to make, but you will need to take the time factor into account, as the fruit purées have to be made then frozen for at least 4 hours, before piping to serve.

You will need to start this recipe at least 4 hours ahead

avocado and lime

3 large avocados (960g), halved, stone removed, chopped

$1/3$ cup (80ml) freshly squeezed lime juice

$2/3$ cup (105g) vegan icing sugar, sifted

1 tsp finely grated lime zest

banana and raspberry

200g frozen raspberries

800g overripe bananas, peeled, coarsely chopped

mango and passionfruit

900g frozen diced mango

$1/4$ cup (60g) passionfruit pulp

1 To make the avocado and lime soft serve, process the avocado, lime juice, and icing sugar until very smooth. Pour the purée into a large resealable bag; seal. Freeze flat for 4 hours or until the purée is solid. Break the frozen purée into chunks, and process until smooth. Spoon the soft serve into a piping bag fitted with a star tube. Immediately pipe the mixture into cups or ice-cream cones; sprinkle with the lime zest to serve. (Makes $2^1/2$ cups)

2 To make the banana and raspberry soft serve, put the frozen raspberries in a food processor; pulse quickly and briefly to roughly crumble. Remove a quarter of the raspberries; reserve in the freezer until ready to serve. Add the banana to the remaining raspberries; process until very smooth. Pour into a large resealable bag; seal. Freeze flat for 4 hours or until the purée is solid. Break the frozen purée into chunks, and process until smooth. Spoon the soft serve into a piping bag fitted with a star tube. Immediately pipe the mixture into cups or ice-cream cones; sprinkle with the frozen crumbled raspberries to serve. (Makes $2^1/2$ cups)

3 To make the mango and passionfruit soft serve, process the mango until very smooth. Add half of the passionfruit pulp; pulse until well combined. Pour into a large resealable bag; seal. Freeze flat for 4 hours or until the purée is solid. Break the frozen purée into chunks, and process until smooth. Spoon the soft serve into a piping bag fitted with a star tube. Immediately pipe the mixture into small cups or ice-cream cones. Drizzle with the remaining passionfruit pulp to serve. (Makes $3^1/2$ cups)

TIPS

• To pipe the soft serves, you will need 3 disposable piping bags and 3 star tubes.

• The soft serve can be stored in the piping bags in the freezer for up to 2 hours before becoming too firm to pipe.

Overnight jasmine tea and lemon curd scrolls

PREP + COOK TIME **45 MINUTES + OVERNIGHT REFRIGERATION** | MAKES **12**

The tea-infused dough for these pull-apart scrolls is left to rise slowly in the fridge overnight, before being shaped and baked the next day.

You will need to start this recipe a day ahead

3 green tea with jasmine teabags

1 tsp finely grated lemon zest, plus extra, to serve

2 tbsp pure maple syrup

3 cups (480g) bread flour

1 tsp (4g) dried yeast

1 1/2 tsp sea salt flakes

1 tsp ground cardamom

chopped pistachios, to serve (optional)

nut filling

1/2 cup (70g) pistachios, coarsely chopped

1/2 cup (40g) shredded coconut, toasted

1/2 cup (110g) firmly packed soft brown sugar

lemon curd

1/3 cup (80ml) lemon juice

1 tbsp cornflour

270ml can coconut cream

1/4 cup (60ml) pure maple syrup

2 pinches of ground turmeric

1   Put the jasmine green tea teabags in a heatproof jug with 1 2/3 cups (410ml) boiling water. Steep for 30 minutes or until the water is lukewarm. Remove the teabags; discard. Stir the 1 teaspoon lemon zest and 1 tablespoon of the maple syrup into the tea.

2   Combine the flour, yeast, sea salt, and cardamom in a large bowl. Make a well in the centre. Pour the tea mixture into the well; mix to a sticky dough. Transfer the dough to a large oiled bowl; cover with cling film. Refrigerate for 12 hours or overnight.

3   Make the nut filling. Combine the ingredients in a small bowl.

4   Turn out the dough onto a well-floured work surface; press out to a 24cm x 40cm rectangle. Scatter with the nut filling. Starting from one long end, tightly roll up the dough to enclose the filling. Cut the log into 12 equal pieces. Place each piece, cut-side up and 1.5cm apart (the mixture will spread), in a greased 25cm springform cake tin. Cover loosely with oiled cling film. Allow to stand in a warm place for 1 hour or until the dough has increased in size by one-third.

5   Meanwhile, make the lemon curd. Whisk the lemon juice and cornflour in a small saucepan over a medium heat until smooth. Whisk in the coconut cream, maple syrup, and turmeric until combined; cook, whisking continuously, until the mixture boils and thickens slightly. Reduce the heat slightly; continue whisking for a further 5 minutes or until the mixture is thick enough to coat the back of a spoon. Transfer to a bowl; cover the surface directly with cling film. Chill until needed.

6   Preheat the oven to 200°C (180°C fan/400°F/Gas 6). Bake the scrolls for 25 minutes. Brush the tops with the remaining 1 tablespoon maple syrup; bake for a further 5 minutes or until shiny and glossy.

7   Drizzle the scrolls with 2 tablespoons of the lemon curd; top with extra grated lemon zest and chopped pistachios, if you like. Serve with the remaining lemon curd.

Coconut and strawberry 'panna cotta'

PREP + COOK TIME **25 MINUTES + REFRIGERATION** | SERVES **4**

A very vegan version of panna cotta, this fresh-flavoured dessert has only four ingredients and can be made ahead of time if you are entertaining. Serve it in glasses or jars, so that the lovely pastel shades of the coconut and strawberry layers are seen to best effect.

4 young drinking coconuts (4kg in total) (see tips)

1/2 tsp agar-agar powder (see tips)

250g strawberries

1 tbsp freshly squeezed lemon juice

unsprayed edible flowers (optional)

1 Place one of the coconuts on its side on a chopping board; carefully cut off the dome-shaped top with a cleaver or large knife – you will need to use a bit of force. Drain the coconut water into a large jug. Spoon out the soft flesh. Repeat with the remaining coconuts; you should end up with about 2 cups (280g) of flesh.

2 Using a high-powered blender, blend the coconut flesh with 1 cup (250ml) of the coconut water until as smooth as possible, to form a purée.

3 Combine 1 cup (250ml) of the coconut water (reserve any leftover coconut water for another use) and the agar-agar powder in a small saucepan. Bring to a simmer, stirring, over a low heat; simmer for 5 minutes. Add to the coconut purée; blend until well combined.

4 Pour two-thirds of the coconut purée into four 1-cup (250ml) glasses or jars, dividing the mixture evenly. Refrigerate for 10 minutes or until slightly set.

5 Reserve half of the strawberries for serving; refrigerate. Hull the remaining strawberries; add to the remaining coconut purée with the juice. Blend until as smooth as possible. Carefully pour over the set coconut mixture; refrigerate for 4 hours or until both layers are set.

6 Serve topped with the reserved sliced or halved strawberries and edible flowers, if you like.

TIPS

- If you don't have access to coconuts, you can use 2 cups (280g) fresh coconut and 2 cups (500ml) coconut water instead.
- Agar-agar powder is available from large supermarkets, health food shops, and online; derived from seaweed, it is a vegan/vegetarian substitute for gelatine.
- You can store the 'panna cotta' in the fridge for up to 4 days.

Ginger, coconut, and almond slice

PREP + COOK TIME **45 MINUTES + STANDING + REFRIGERATION** | MAKES **16**

Ginger lovers rejoice! This vegan-friendly slice is layered with creamy coconut and topped with toasted flaked almonds and crystallized ginger. Use the leftover coconut water as a base for fruity summer drinks, for cooking rice, or in Berry Basket Cream Tarts (page 172).

You will need to start this recipe a day ahead

1½ cups (225g) raw cashews

1 young drinking coconut (1.2kg)

1½ cups (240g) natural almonds

1 cup (140g) pitted dried dates, coarsely chopped

½ cup (40g) shredded coconut

¾ cup (165g) crystallized ginger, thinly sliced

¾ cup (180ml) melted coconut oil

½ cup (125ml) rice malt syrup

2 tbsp finely grated fresh root ginger

½ cup (125ml) coconut milk

1½ tsp vanilla extract

2 tbsp flaked almonds, toasted, to serve

1   Put the cashews in a medium bowl; cover with cold water. Allow to stand, covered, for 1 hour. Drain the cashews, rinse under cold water; drain well.

2   Line the bottom and sides of a 23cm square cake tin with baking parchment, extending the parchment 5cm over the sides.

3   Place the coconut on its side on a chopping board; carefully cut off the dome-shaped top with a cleaver or large knife – you will need to use a bit of force. Drain the coconut water into a large jug (reserve the coconut water for another use). Spoon out the soft coconut flesh; you should have about ½ cup (90g).

4   Process the drained cashews and almonds until finely chopped. Add the dates, shredded coconut, ¼ cup (55g) of the crystallized ginger, ¼ cup (60ml) of the coconut oil and 1 tablespoon of the rice malt syrup; pulse until combined. Press the mixture over the bottom of the prepared tin. Refrigerate until needed.

5   Blend or process the fresh coconut, fresh root ginger, coconut milk, vanilla extract, the remaining coconut oil, the remaining rice malt syrup, and ¼ cup (55g) of the crystallized ginger until smooth. Pour the mixture over the biscuit base. Refrigerate the slice overnight.

6   Cut the slice into pieces; serve topped with the flaked almonds and remaining ¼ cup (55g) crystallized ginger.

TIP

The slice keeps well in an airtight container in the fridge for up to 1 week, or can be frozen for up to 2 months; thaw in the fridge.

Peppermint bites

PREP TIME **45 MINUTES + STANDING, FREEZING + REFRIGERATION** | MAKES **15**

Buckwheat groats add crunch to these no-bake beauties. Make sure to use peppermint extract, rather than oil or essence; otherwise the flavour of the biscuits may be affected.

You will need to start this recipe a day ahead

³/₄ cup (115g) raw cashews

¹/₂ cup (80g) natural almonds

¹/₂ cup (60g) pecans

¹/₃ cup (65g) activated buckwheat groats (see tips)

²/₃ cup (50g) desiccated coconut

¹/₂ cup (50g) cacao powder

¹/₄ cup (40g) coconut sugar

2 tsp mesquite powder (see tips)

4 soft fresh dates (80g), pitted

²/₃ cup (140g) coconut oil, melted

¹/₄ cup (60ml) coconut cream

2 tbsp light agave syrup

¹/₂ tsp pure peppermint extract (see tips)

chocolate coating

¹/₄ cup (50g) coconut oil

60g cacao butter, chopped

2 tbsp pure maple syrup

¹/₂ cup (50g) cacao powder

TIPS

• Activated buckwheat groats (buckinis) and mesquite powder are available from some health food shops, wholefood grocers, and online.
• Use peppermint extract, available from health food shops, rather than oil or essence; otherwise the biscuits' flavour may be affected.
• Store the biscuits in an airtight container in the fridge for up to 5 days.

1 Put the cashews in a medium bowl; cover with cold water. Allow to stand, covered, for 4 hours or overnight. Drain the cashews, rinse under cold water; drain well.

2 Lightly grease a 20cm x 30cm slice or shallow rectangular cake tin; line with cling film, extending the cling film 5cm over the sides.

3 Process the almonds, pecans, buckwheat groats, desiccated coconut, cacao powder, coconut sugar, mesquite powder, dates, and ¹/₂ cup (125ml) of the coconut oil until coarse crumbs form and the mixture starts to clump. Be careful not to over-process. Press the mixture firmly and evenly over the bottom of the tin, using a spatula to form a 5mm thick layer. Freeze for 15 minutes or until firm.

4 Lift the biscuit base from the tin; place on a board. Cut the base into 15 rounds using a 5cm biscuit cutter. Place the rounds on a tray lined with baking parchment; freeze while preparing the peppermint cream.

5 To make the peppermint cream, blend the drained cashews with the remaining coconut oil, coconut cream, and agave syrup until as smooth as possible. (If you have one, use a high-powered blender, for a very smooth consistency.) Add the peppermint extract; blend until combined. Pour the peppermint cream into a small bowl. Cover, then freeze, stirring occasionally, for 1 hour or until thick but not set.

6 Spoon 2 teaspoons of peppermint cream onto each biscuit round; using the back of the teaspoon, gently press down to flatten and smooth. Freeze for 3 hours or until set.

7 Make the chocolate coating. Put the coconut oil and cacao butter in a medium heatproof bowl over a smaller heatproof bowl of boiling water, whisk until combined and smooth; whisk in the maple syrup. Whisk in the cacao powder until combined and smooth. Pour into a small bowl.

8 Using a fork, lower the biscuits, one at a time, into the chocolate mixture. Allow any excess chocolate to drain off, then place each biscuit on the tray. Refrigerate for 30 minutes or until the chocolate is set.

Berry basket cream tarts

PREP + COOK TIME **50 MINUTES + STANDING, COOLING + REFRIGERATION** | MAKES **6**

These luscious nut-cream-filled tarts are the answer to all vegan dreams of being able to eat a beautiful creamy French-style fruit tart. Choose the best, most perfectly ripe fruit you can find to top the tarts, to make the most of their taste and aroma.

You will need to start this recipe at least 4 hours ahead

2 cups (320g) natural almonds

¾ cup (100g) pitted medjool dates

20g coconut oil, melted

1 tbsp psyllium husks

1–2 tbsp coconut water

125g fresh raspberries

½ cup (65g) small strawberries, halved

½ cup (75g) fresh blueberries

½ cup (100g) cherries, halved

¼ cup unsprayed edible flowers (optional)

pastry cream

2½ cups (350g) raw macadamias

⅔ cup (160ml) agave syrup

¾ cup (180ml) coconut water

2 tsp finely grated orange zest

2 tsp vanilla bean paste

¾ cup (150g) coconut oil, melted

1 Preheat the oven to 160°C (140°C fan/325°F/Gas 3). Grease six 12cm mini pie dishes; line the bottoms and sides of each with 2 strips of baking parchment to form a cross, extending the strips over the sides.

2 Make the pastry cream. Put the macadamias in a medium bowl; cover with cold water. Allow to stand for 4 hours or overnight; drain. Rinse the macadamias; drain well. Put the soaked macadamias into the jug of a high-powered blender with the remaining ingredients for the pastry cream; blend until smooth. (Using a high-powered blender will give very smooth results.)

3 Process the almonds, dates, coconut oil, psyllium husks, and enough of the coconut water to ensure the mixture forms a coarse paste and clumps together.

4 Press ⅓ cup of the nut mixture firmly over bottom and side of each pie dish. Place the dishes on a large baking tray. Bake for 15 minutes or until lightly browned; allow to cool.

5 Carefully remove the tart cases from the dishes; place on a large tray. Divide the pastry cream evenly among the cases. Cover, then refrigerate for 4 hours or overnight until set.

6 Serve the tarts topped with the fresh fruit and sprinkled with edible flowers, if you like.

TIP

The tarts can be made a day ahead; keep, covered, in the fridge. Decorate with the berries and flowers, if using, just before serving.

Rice pudding with poached rhubarb and plums

PREP + COOK TIME **50 MINUTES + COOLING** | SERVES **6**

Wonderfully versatile, rice pudding makes for a perfect dessert. You can even serve this vegan-friendly version for brunch, if you like. Rich and creamy thanks to oat milk and coconut syrup, it's topped with sweet poached rhubarb and plums for a vibrant touch.

2 tbsp pistachios

3 oranges (720g in total)

2 tbsp vegan margarine spread

3/4 cup (160g) sushi rice

1 litre (4 cups) oat milk or other dairy-free milk (see tips)

1/3 cup (80ml) coconut syrup

2 tsp vanilla bean paste

poached rhubarb and plums

1 litre (4 cups) apple juice

2 tbsp coconut syrup

1 cinnamon stick

4 star anise

3 large rhubarb stems (300g), trimmed, cut into 7cm lengths

4 small blood plums (300g), quartered, seeded

TIPS

• You can use any dairy-free milk, except for almond milk, for the rice pudding. Oat milk is a good choice, as is coconut milk – although you may need a little more, as this is thicker than other dairy-free milks.

• If the stems of the rhubarb are thin, reduce the cooking time accordingly.

• The rice pudding and poached fruit can be made a day ahead; keep refrigerated, separately, until needed. Reheat the rice pudding with a little more of your chosen dairy-free milk for a creamy mixture.

1 Make the poached rhubarb and plums. Bring the apple juice, coconut syrup, cinnamon, and star anise to a simmer in a medium saucepan over a medium heat. Add the rhubarb and plums; simmer, uncovered, for 2 minutes. Be careful not to boil the fruit or it will be mushy. Remove the fruit from the pan with a slotted spoon; transfer to a heatproof bowl. Peel the plums; discard the skin. Bring the syrup to the boil, then reduce the heat and simmer, uncovered, for 30 minutes or until reduced to 1 cup (250ml). Allow to cool slightly. Serve warm.

2 Meanwhile, preheat the oven to 180°C (160°C fan/350°F/Gas 4). Spread the pistachios over a baking tray; roast for 5 minutes or until lightly browned. (Or, put the pistachios in a frying pan; toast over a low-medium heat, stirring, until lightly browned.)

3 Remove the zest from one of the oranges using a zester. (Or, peel the zest thinly from the orange, avoiding the white pith. Cut the zest into long, thin strips.) Set aside until needed. Squeeze the juice from the oranges; you will need 1 cup (250ml).

4 Melt the vegan margarine in a large deep frying pan over a medium heat. Add the sushi rice; cook, stirring, for 2 minutes. Add the orange juice, oat milk, coconut syrup, and vanilla bean paste; bring to the boil. Reduce the heat to a simmer. Cook, uncovered, stirring occasionally, for 20 minutes or until the rice is tender and the mixture is thick.

5 Spoon the rice mixture into six 11/2-cup (375ml) bowls. Serve topped with the poached fruit and warm fruit syrup, sprinkled with toasted pistachios and reserved orange zest.

Fudgy sweet potato brownies with espresso sauce

PREP + COOK TIME **1 HOUR 30 MINUTES** | MAKES **16**

Grind the linseed (flaxseed) for these gooey brownies yourself, or make sure to buy it from shops or supermarkets with a good turnover, as ground linseed turns rancid quite quickly.

1 orange sweet potato (400g), peeled, chopped

2 tbsp ground linseed (milled flaxseed)

1/2 cup (125ml) hot water

180g vegan dark chocolate (70% cocoa), chopped

1 1/4 cups (200g) coconut sugar

2 tsp vanilla extract

2 tbsp cacao powder

1 cup (120g) ground almonds

1/4 tsp bicarbonate of soda

espresso sauce

2 tsp instant coffee granules

1 tbsp boiling water

1/3 cup (80ml) pure maple syrup

1/3 cup (55g) coconut sugar

20g vegan dark chocolate (70% cocoa), chopped

1/4 cup (50g) coconut oil

2 tsp vanilla extract

1/4 cup (25g) cacao powder

TIPS

• The sauce thickens quickly on standing. Reheat gently to return to a thin consistency.

• These brownies are delicious at room temperature and last for up to 3 days in an airtight container in the fridge. Bring to room temperature before serving. They can also be frozen for up to 2 months.

1 Put the sweet potato in a medium saucepan with enough cold water to cover; bring to the boil. Cook, covered, for 15 minutes or until soft. Drain; return to the saucepan. Mash until smooth.

2 Meanwhile, preheat the oven to 180°C (160°C fan/350°F/Gas 4). Lightly grease a deep 20cm square cake tin with cooking spray; line the bottom with baking parchment.

3 Combine the ground linseed and the hot water in a small heatproof bowl. Allow to stand for 10 minutes.

4 Put the chocolate, coconut sugar, vanilla extract, 1/4 cup (60ml) water, and sifted cacao powder in a large heatproof bowl over a saucepan of simmering water. Stir until melted and smooth. Remove from the heat; stir in the mashed sweet potato. Add the linseed mixture, ground almonds, and bicarbonate of soda; mix well. Pour the mixture into the prepared cake tin. Bake for 1 hour or until firm to the touch. Allow to cool slightly in the tin.

5 Make the espresso sauce. Dissolve the coffee in the boiling water. Combine the maple syrup, coconut sugar, chocolate, coconut oil, vanilla extract, and coffee in a small saucepan over a low heat; stir until melted and smooth. Remove from the heat; stir in the sifted cacao powder.

6 Cut the warm brownie into squares. Serve with the espresso sauce, topped with sweet potato peace signs, if you like (see below).

peace-sign brownies To decorate the brownie squares with individual sweet potato peace signs, peel and slice 1 small orange sweet potato (300g) into 3mm thick slices. Using a 3cm pastry cutter, cut into rounds. Heat 2 teaspoons coconut oil in a large frying pan over a high heat, then cook the sweet potato for 2 minutes on each side until just tender. Pour in 1 tablespoon coconut syrup, and cook for another minute until slightly caramelized. Cut each sweet potato round into peace symbols, as pictured opposite.

Caramel coconut bread pudding

PREP + COOK TIME **1 HOUR + STANDING** | SERVES **6**

This humble bread pudding is incredibly satisfying, easy to make, and tastes heavenly.
Serve warm or cooled, with a drizzle of rich caramel sauce to top it all off.

1/2 cup (80g) coconut sugar

1 cup (250ml) coconut cream

2 tbsp pure maple syrup

3 tsp cornflour

2 tsp vanilla extract

2 cups (500ml) almond milk

1/2 cup (125g) apple sauce

1/2 tsp mixed spice

620g loaf of wholemeal sourdough bread, crusts removed, coarsely chopped

1/3 cup (55g) sultanas

1/2 cup (60g) pecans

1/2 cup (25g) coconut flakes, toasted (see tips)

1 Combine 1/3 cup (55g) of the coconut sugar, 2/3 cup (180ml) of the coconut cream, maple syrup, cornflour, and 1 teaspoon of the vanilla extract in a small saucepan; stir until smooth. Cook, stirring, over a medium heat until the mixture boils and thickens. Remove from the heat.

2 Transfer half of the coconut caramel sauce to a large heatproof jug (set aside the rest). Gradually stir in the almond milk, apple sauce, mixed spice, and the remaining 1 teaspoon vanilla extract.

3 Preheat the oven to 180°C (160°C fan/350°F/Gas 4). Grease a 2-litre (8-cup) 22cm x 30cm baking dish. Layer the bread, sultanas, and pecans in the dish. Pour the milk mixture over the bread, making sure that all the bread is soaked. Allow to stand for 15 minutes.

4 Sprinkle the bread with the remaining coconut sugar. Bake the pudding for 40 minutes or until set.

5 Serve the pudding warm or cooled, with the reserved caramel sauce, remaining coconut cream, and toasted coconut flakes.

TIPS

- To toast the coconut, stir continuously in a heavy-based frying pan over a medium heat for 3 minutes or until lightly browned and toasted.
- If the reserved caramel sauce becomes a little thick on standing, stir in some extra coconut cream or almond milk, and reheat gently over a low heat to return to a sauce consistency.

Chocolate ganache cupcakes

PREP + COOK TIME **45 MINUTES + COOLING + REFRIGERATION** | MAKES **12**

Fancify the cupcakes with colourful extras, such as beetroot powder and smashed pistachio, squares of colourful vegan chocolate, or pretty edible flowers, if you like. Or decorate as pictured here, using dehydrated pear and raspberry powder (see tips).

3/4 cup (180ml) soy milk

2 tsp apple cider vinegar

1/2 cup (110g) caster sugar

1/4 cup (60ml) vegetable oil

1 tsp vanilla extract

3/4 cup (110g) self-raising flour

1/4 cup (25g) cocoa powder

1/2 tsp bicarbonate of soda

1 tsp baking powder

1/2 teaspoon salt

chocolate ganache

200g vegan dark chocolate (70% cocoa), chopped

3/4 cup (180ml) canned coconut cream

1 tsp vanilla extract

1 tsp sea salt

1 Preheat the oven to 180°C (160°C fan/350°F/Gas 4). Line a 12-hole (1/3-cup/80ml) muffin tin with paper cases.

2 Whisk together the soy milk and vinegar in a large bowl. Allow to stand for 5 minutes to curdle. Add the caster sugar, vegetable oil, and vanilla extract to the soy mixture; whisk until foamy.

3 Sift the dry ingredients onto a sheet of baking parchment. Sift again over the milk mixture, in 2 batches, then whisk until almost smooth. Spoon the mixture into the cases. Bake for 18 minutes or until a skewer inserted into the centre comes out clean. Transfer the cupcakes to a wire rack to cool.

4 Meanwhile, make the chocolate ganache. Put the chocolate in a medium heatproof bowl over a saucepan of simmering water. Stir until the chocolate is smooth; remove from the heat. Stir in the coconut cream, vanilla extract, and sea salt. Refrigerate, whisking every 10 minutes, for 30 minutes or until spreadable.

5 Serve the cupcakes topped with the ganache.

TIPS

- The cupcakes can be baked up to 2 days ahead; store in an airtight container at room temperature.
- You can freeze the cupcakes, without ganache, for up to 3 months.
- Decorate with dehydrated sliced pear arranged on top of the cupcakes, sprinkled with raspberry powder. Soak the pear in raspberry juice to make the cupcakes even more decadent, if you like.

Raw tiramisu

PREP TIME **45 MINUTES + STANDING, REFRIGERATION + FREEZING** | MAKES **6**

Vegan, sugar-free, and dairy-free, this creamy raw tiramisu is a modern take on the Italian classic. You can use espresso, cold-drip, percolator, or plunger coffee for the recipe.

You will need to start this recipe a day ahead

2 cups (300g) raw cashews

1½ cups (120g) desiccated coconut

¾ cup (75g) hazelnut meal

½ cup (60g) ground almonds

¼ cup (20g) psyllium husks

¼ cup (60ml) coconut milk

¼ cup (60ml) coconut nectar

½ tsp vanilla extract

2 tbsp espresso coffee

2 tsp pure maple syrup

¼ cup (25g) cacao powder, plus extra, to decorate

coffee cream

½ cup (125ml) coconut cream

¼ cup (60ml) pure maple syrup

¼ cup (50g) coconut oil, melted

⅓ cup (80ml) espresso coffee

1 tsp pure vanilla extract

vanilla cream

¾ cup (180ml) coconut cream

¼ cup (60ml) pure maple syrup

¼ cup (50g) coconut oil, melted

2 tsp vanilla extract

TIPS

- If you have one, use a high-powered blender in steps 5 and 7, to achieve a very smooth consistency.
- Store in a container in the fridge for up to 4 days.

1 Put the cashews in a medium bowl; cover with cold water. Allow to stand, covered, for 4 hours or overnight. Drain the cashews, then rinse under cold water; drain well. Reserve for the coffee cream and vanilla cream.

2 Lightly grease a 20cm x 30cm shallow rectangular cake tin; line the bottom and long sides with baking parchment, extending the parchment 5cm over the sides.

3 To make the 'sponge', blend the desiccated coconut until finely ground; transfer to a large bowl. Stir in the hazelnut meal, ground almonds, and psyllium husks. Whisk together the coconut milk, coconut nectar, and vanilla extract in a small bowl. Add to the dry ingredients; mix until well combined. Press the sponge mixture evenly over the bottom of the tin. Refrigerate for 30 minutes to firm up slightly.

4 Meanwhile, whisk together the coffee and maple syrup in a small bowl until combined.

5 Make the coffee cream. Blend half of the reserved cashews with all the ingredients until as smooth as possible.

6 Cut twelve 6cm rounds from the sponge. Reserve and refrigerate 6 rounds. Dip 6 rounds, one at a time, into the coffee syrup. Lightly press into the bottoms of six 1-cup (250ml) glasses or jars. Don't worry if the sponge breaks up. Pour half of the coffee cream over the sponge bases; dust with sifted cacao powder. Freeze for 15 minutes to firm up slightly.

7 To make the vanilla cream, blend the remaining cashews with all the ingredients until as smooth as possible. Pour half of the vanilla cream over the coffee cream layer; dust with sifted cacao powder. Freeze for 10 minutes to firm up slightly.

8 Repeat the layering with the reserved sponge rounds dipped in coffee syrup, coffee cream, sifted cacao powder, vanilla cream, and sifted cacao powder, freezing between layers. Cover; refrigerate for 6 hours or until firm. Dust with a little extra sifted cacao powder before serving.

Coconut scones

PREP + COOK TIME **40 MINUTES + COOLING & REFRIGERATION** | MAKES **12**

It's hard to pass up a good, simple scone, and these don't disappoint. A fresh look at an old favourite, they are completely vegan and use soda water to help keep them light and fluffy. Just remember – don't overmix the dough and stamp out, not twist, the rounds.

3 cups (450g) self-raising flour

$^1/_4$ cup (40g) vegan icing sugar

$^3/_4$ cup (180ml) canned coconut milk, plus extra 1 tbsp

1 cup (250ml) soda water

125g fresh raspberries

1 tsp lemon juice

3 tsp coconut sugar

1 cup (280g) dairy-free coconut yogurt (use Home-made Coconut Yogurt on page 21 or buy ready-made)

1 Preheat the oven to 220°C (200°C fan/425°F/Gas 7). Line a baking tray with baking parchment.

2 Sift together the flour and icing sugar into a large bowl. Make a well in the centre; add the $^3/_4$ cup (180ml) coconut milk and soda water. Use a butter knife to 'cut' the liquid through the flour mixture, mixing to a soft, sticky dough. Turn out onto a lightly floured work surface; working quickly, knead until just smooth. Press out the dough to a 3cm thickness.

3 Dip a 5.5cm biscuit cutter in flour; cut 12 rounds from the dough. Place the scones side by side on the prepared tray, just touching. Brush the tops of the scones with the extra 1 tablespoon coconut milk. Bake for 15 minutes or until browned and the centre scones sound hollow when tapped. Leave the scones on the tray for 3 minutes, before transferring to a wire rack to cool.

4 Put the raspberries, lemon juice, and coconut sugar in a medium bowl. Using a fork, crush the raspberries. Refrigerate for 30 minutes. Drain the excess liquid from the raspberries over a jug or bowl.

5 Halve the cooled scones; serve topped with the coconut yogurt and the berry mixture.

TIPS

• You can use a smaller cutter and make smaller scones if you like; reduce the cooking time slightly.

• These scones are best made on the day of serving, but they can also be frozen in a container for up to 2 months. To thaw the scones, wrap in foil and heat in the oven at 180°C (160°C fan/350°F/Gas 4) for 10 minutes or until heated through.

Loaded hot chocolates

Rich and indulgent, these vegan-friendly hot chocolates are almost desserts in themselves. What better way could there be to keep toasty warm on a chilly night than to snuggle into a comfortable seat and slowly sip and savour one of these gems?

Persian chocolate

PREP + COOK TIME **15 MINUTES** | SERVES **2**

Pit and finely chop 8 medjool dates (160g). Put ¼ cup Dutch-process cocoa powder and ¼ teaspoon ground cardamom in a medium deep saucepan; slowly whisk in 2½ cups (625ml) almond milk until well combined. Add the chopped dates; slowly bring to the boil over a low heat. Using a hand-held blender, blend on low speed until smooth. Add 1 teaspoon vanilla bean paste and 2 teaspoons rosewater; stir until combined. (Taste the mixture and adjust the amount of rosewater, if needed, as brands vary.) Pour into 2 large mugs. Top each mug with a handful of rose-flavoured pashmak (Persian candyfloss; use vegan candyfloss if you can't find this), topped with 2 tablespoons slivered pistachios, 1 tablespoon cocoa nibs, and edible dried rose petals, if you like.

Spiced and spiked chocolate

PREP + COOK TIME **20 MINUTES + COOLING** | SERVES **2**

Put ½ cup (125ml) water, ¼ orange, peeled and sliced, 2 whole star anise, ¼ cup (60g) firmly packed soft brown sugar, and ⅓ cup (80ml) spiced rum in a small saucepan; simmer gently over a low heat until syrupy. Remove the star anise and orange slices; discard. Stir in 150g finely chopped vegan dark chocolate until melted and smooth. Stir in 2 cups (500ml) almond milk; bring to a simmer, stirring occasionally. Pour into 2 large mugs. Top with a generous scoop of dairy-free vanilla ice cream; dust with cocoa powder, and sprinkle with finely grated orange zest.

Salted white caramel

PREP + COOK TIME **15 MINUTES** | SERVES **2**

Sprinkle ⅓ cup (75g) caster sugar and ½ teaspoon crumbled sea salt flakes over the bottom of a medium heavy-based saucepan. Place the pan over a low-medium heat; cook without stirring until the sugar dissolves and forms a golden caramel. Immediately add 20g coconut oil and ½ cup (125ml) coconut cream; stir until the caramel melts. Remove from the heat; remove ¼ cup (60ml) of the caramel mixture. Gradually stir 2 cups (500ml) almond milk and 2 teaspoons cornflour into the remaining caramel mixture in the pan; cook, stirring, until the mixture boils and thickens slightly. Pour into 2 large mugs. Top with a dollop of whipped coconut cream and the reserved caramel. Scatter with caramel popcorn, if you like.

Thick Spanish-style chocolate

PREP + COOK TIME **15 MINUTES** | SERVES **2**

Pour 2½ cups (625ml) almond milk into a medium saucepan with 2 cinnamon sticks. Remove 2 tablespoons milk from the pan; stir together with 3 teaspoons cornflour in a small cup to a smooth paste. Slowly bring the milk almost to the boil over a low heat, so that the milk has time to absorb the cinnamon flavour. Add 150g finely chopped vegan dark chocolate, the cornflour mixture, and a pinch of chilli powder; whisk until the chocolate melts and the mixture boils and thickens slightly. Discard the cinnamon. Pour into 2 large mugs. Top with extra grated vegan dark chocolate, dust with cocoa and a pinch of ground chilli.

Conversion chart

A note on Australian measures

- One Australian metric measuring cup holds approximately 250ml.

- One Australian metric tablespoon holds 20ml.

- One Australian metric teaspoon holds 5ml.

- The difference between one country's measuring cups and another's is within a two- or three-teaspoon variance, and should not affect your cooking results.

- North America, New Zealand, and the United Kingdom use a 15ml tablespoon.

Using measures in this book

- All cup and spoon measurements are level.

- The most accurate way of measuring dry ingredients is to weigh them.

- When measuring liquids, use a clear glass or plastic jug with metric markings.

- All fruit and vegetables are assumed to be medium unless otherwise stated.

Dry measures

metric	imperial
15g	$1/2$oz
30g	1oz
60g	2oz
90g	3oz
125g	4oz ($1/4$lb)
155g	5oz
185g	6oz
220g	7oz
250g	8oz ($1/2$lb)
280g	9oz
315g	10oz
345g	11oz
375g	12oz ($3/4$lb)
410g	13oz
440g	14oz
470g	15oz
500g	16oz (1lb)
750g	24oz ($1^1/2$lb)
1kg	32oz (2lb)

Liquid measures

metric	imperial
30ml	1 fluid oz
60ml	2 fluid oz
100ml	3 fluid oz
125ml	4 fluid oz
150ml	5 fluid oz
190ml	6 fluid oz
250ml	8 fluid oz
300ml	10 fluid oz
500ml	16 fluid oz
600ml	20 fluid oz
1000ml (1 litre)	$1^3/4$ pints

Length measures

metric	imperial
3mm	$1/8$in
6mm	$1/4$in
1cm	$1/2$in
2cm	$3/4$in
2.5cm	1in
5cm	2in
6cm	$2^1/2$in
8cm	3in
10cm	4in
13cm	5in
15cm	6in
18cm	7in
20cm	8in
22cm	9in
25cm	10in
28cm	11in
30cm	12in (1ft)

Oven temperatures

The oven temperatures in this book are for conventional ovens; if you have a fan-forced oven, decrease the temperature by 10–20 degrees.

	°C (Celsius)	°F (Fahrenheit)
Very slow	120	250
Slow	150	300
Moderately slow	160	325
Moderate	180	350
Moderately hot	200	400
Hot	220	425
Very hot	240	475

Index

Acknowledgments

DK would like to thank Sophia Young, Joe Reville, Amanda Chebatte, and Georgia Moore for their assistance in making this book.

The Australian Women's Weekly Test Kitchen in Sydney has developed, tested, and photographed the recipes in this book.